Jürgen Beyerer, Alexey Pak (Eds.)

Proceedings of the 2014 Joint Workshop of Fraunhofer IOSB and Institute for Anthropomatics, Vision and Fusion Laboratory

Karlsruher Schriften zur Anthropomatik
Band 20
Herausgeber: Prof. Dr.-Ing. Jürgen Beyerer

Lehrstuhl für Interaktive Echtzeitsysteme
Karlsruher Institut für Technologie

Fraunhofer-Institut für Optronik, Systemtechnik und
Bildauswertung IOSB Karlsruhe

Eine Übersicht aller bisher in dieser Schriftenreihe erschienenen Bände finden Sie am Ende des Buchs.

Proceedings of the 2014 Joint Workshop of Fraunhofer IOSB and Institute for Anthropomatics, Vision and Fusion Laboratory

Edited by
Jürgen Beyerer
Alexey Pak

KIT Scientific Publishing

Impressum

KIT Scientific Publishing

Karlsruher Institut für Technologie (KIT)
KIT Scientific Publishing
Straße am Forum 2
D-76131 Karlsruhe

KIT Scientific Publishing is a registered trademark of Karlsruhe Institute of Technology. Reprint using the book cover is not allowed.

www.ksp.kit.edu

Print on Demand 2015

ISSN 1863-6489
ISBN 978-3-7315-0401-6
DOI 10.5445/KSP/1000047712

Preface

In 2014, the annual joint workshop of the Fraunhofer Institute of Optronics, System Technologies and Image Exploitation (IOSB) and the Vision and Fusion Laboratory (IES) of the Institute for Anthropomatics, Karlsruhe Institute of Technology (KIT) has again been hosted by the town of Triberg-Nussbach in Germany.

For a week from July, 20 to 26 the PhD students of the both institutions delivered extended reports on the status of their research and participated in thorough discussions on topics ranging from computer vision and world modeling to data fusion and human-machine interaction. Most results and ideas presented at the workshop are collected in this book in the form of detailed technical reports. This volume provides a comprehensive and up-to-date overview of the research program of the IES Laboratory and the Fraunhofer IOSB.

The editors thank Miriam Ruf, Julius Pfrommer and other organizers for their efforts resulting in a pleasant and inspiring atmosphere throughout the week. We would also like to thank the doctoral students for writing and reviewing the technical reports as well as for responding to the comments and the suggestions of their colleagues.

Prof. Dr.-Ing. Jürgen Beyerer
Alexey Pak, PhD

Contents

Automated Microscopy - an Overview Driven by Application 1
Peter Frühberger

Face Recognition 13
Christian Herrmann

Wavelet Methods for Classification of Surface Data 25
Tan-Toan Le

Visual Inspection of Transparent Objects 37
Johannes Meyer

Thickness Measurement of Thin Films 49
Christian Negara

Towards smooth generic camera calibration 67
Alexey Pak

DCOP over Constrained Communication Topologies 77
Julius Pfrommer

3D Facial Texture Extraction Robust to Self-Occlusion 89
Chengchao Qu

Learning discriminative features for visual inspection 103
Matthias Richter

Image Warping and Homogenization for Structural-Statistical Textures 115
Markus Vogelbacher

Defect perception thresholds on specular surfaces 123
Mathias Ziebarth

Automated Microscopy
an overview driven by application

Peter Frühberger

Vision and Fusion Laboratory
Institute for Anthropomatics
Karlsruhe Institute of Technology (KIT), Germany
fruehberger@kit.edu

Technical Report IES-2014-01

Abstract: In this report, the task of automating microscopic inspection techniques in an industrial environment is considered. Approaches are presented, that adapt these techniques for quality assurance (QA) while focusing on integration into already existing industrial processes. The specific limitations of microscopic image acquisition, such as an extremely narrow depth of field, exhibit particular challenges for operating microscopes in an automated way. This image acquisition is the basis of an industrial scale image analysis with decent quality. A subset of possible solutions to selected requirements are discussed. This report suggests novel ways of exploiting microscopic measurements while using multi-sensor fusion as an example to construct a model for 3D estimation by combining 2.5D measurement data and pre-acquired ground-truth a priori data.

1 Introduction

Microscopes are used in a wide field of applications. They are utilized for analyzing medical and biological samples on the one hand, but are also used for industrial quality assurance on the other hand. Microscopic inspection is mostly a manual task done by experts, trained for this specific task. Quality assurance is an important production step when producing technical goods like electronic components. It is obviously clear that in-process quality assurance, while keeping a decent production speed, cannot be done by manual usage of microscopes, rather an automated inspection needs to be implemented.

This work uses off the shelf microscopes, that are controlled automatically while using established components out of the automation industry and automated production. The work is also focusing on the possibilities of integration, hardware and software wise, to combine microscopic analysis with established industrial camera systems in already existing processes. As image processing techniques need to be adapted to microscopic dimensions to compensate a limited depth of view or depth of focus, specific methods are selected. Those methods are needed in order to stitch lateral adjacent images or to reconstruct 3D models out of images that were acquired by a 2D sensor.

The latter approach opens up a second interesting field when working with different microscopes. When computing 3D images out of 2D sensor data, previous knowledge, e.g. ground-truth knowledge can be used in order to build up the constraints of this underlying model. Combining the altitude information of a 3D scanning device with 2D sensor data at hand into a model based image processing approach is to be considered as a multi-sensor data fusion.

2 Task oriented quality assurance

There is a wide range of industrial applications that need microscopic inspection. The requirements therefore are quite different. On the one hand, it is common practice to only inspect specific, selected goods manually. Those goods are picked randomly or depending on characteristic numbers that are deduced from the industrial process itself. An example for random detailed inspection is the functional check of mass produced surface mounted devices (SMD) for inexpensive components. Here the resulting good is rather cheap, the production steps are simple and therefore a 100% inspection would not return the investment. In contrast when producing high quality goods, component suppliers need to guarantee a certain number of defect free working units in order to ensure a continuous production. For this purpose, fast inspection techniques that keep pace with the production are needed. The component of choice therefore are industrial cameras. Those devices can inspect a large field of view when equipped with suitable optics. But industrial cameras have limited application domains. On the one hand, there is a limit of the number of pixels available for such sensors and on the other hand, when choosing optics for very detailed lateral resolutions, the field of view will get a lot smaller, which requires the lateral stitching of parallel or consecutive acquired images, as seen in section 2.2. Especially this latter task motivates the combination of industrial camera systems with microscopes. Those devices are equipped with components like moving tables or a movable z-axis to compensate a limited depth of view and also a limited depth of field by combining multiple acquired images. An example of board inspection with such a combined setup is given in section 2.3.

The limited depth of view can be compensated by acquiring an image stack of different focused images and creating a synthetically enhanced image by estimating the contrast of each input image, which is shown in section 2.1.

2.1 Using 2D focus series to obtain 3D information

When using large magnification, the resulting depth of view is decreasing. When acquiring an image stack by moving the microscope's z-axis, the contrast information of each single image can be used to create a synthetically enhanced image [FKB14]. This estimation - not necessarily being based on a physical model - tries to select specific regions on the image that are in focus. Under ideal conditions, the chosen contrast measure produces high values for those focused regions while returning low values for the remaining ones. In the following approach, a simple contrast measure that is based on an estimated local variance $\hat{\sigma}(x, y)$ is used. It is normalized over the rectangular region $c_r(w, h)$. A low pass filter (LP) is used to estimate the mean value $\hat{\mu}$ of an image region R with height h and width w. It is defined as follows:

$$\hat{\mu}(x, y) = LP\{R(x, y)\}$$
$$\hat{\sigma}(x, y) = \sqrt{LP\{(R(x, y) - \hat{\mu}(x, y))^2\}}$$
$$c_r(w, h) = \frac{1}{h \cdot w} \cdot \sum_{x=0}^{h} \sum_{y=0}^{w} \sigma(x, y)$$

Special emphasize is given to the depth map in figure 2.1(d), that can be used for estimating the relative height differences between the local maxima of the focus measure. This information is useful when a rough height estimation is needed. Depending on the applied focus measure, an accuracy in the lower micrometer range is easily possible as demonstrated in commercial products like the Alicona InfiniteFocus, as shown on figure 3.3.

2.2 Image stitching of microscope images

Stitching of microscope images can become a complex task, especially when the real size of one image pixel gets more detailed (higher resolution) than the accuracy of the positioning stage. This is easily the case for large magnification. Then, invariant features of the image, like edges or other dominant features, need to be

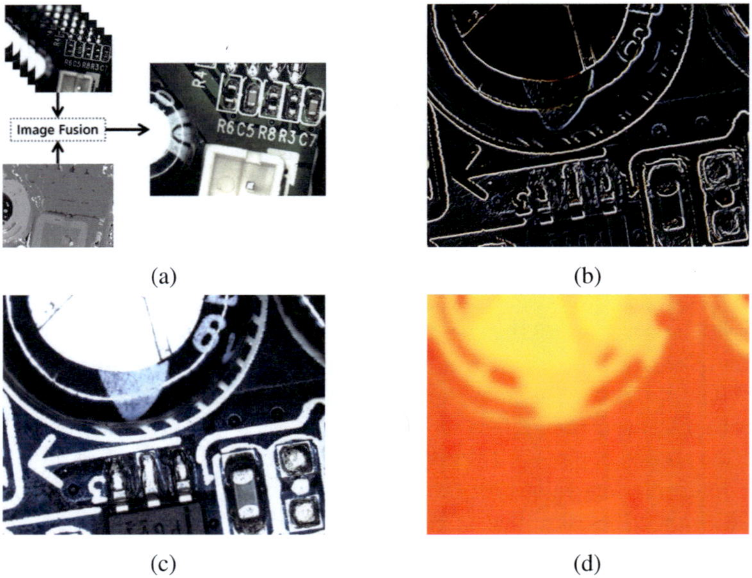

Figure 2.1: An image stack (a) is analyzed and the contrast measure of each image is determined (b). Afterwards this information is used to create a synthetically enhanced image (c). The largest contrast per pixel is stored in a depth map (d), which is used as the second input to generate the enhanced image.

used to estimate a useful stitching result. As the depth of focus is getting very low with large magnification as seen in the previous section 2.1, it is often necessary to perform the feature based image stitching on synthetically enhanced images. As the physical relationship of microscope camera to the moving table only changes into one direction, while assuming the camera is parallel to the positioning stage, only a simple translation vector needs to be estimated. This knowledge can be reused as expert knowledge when adding the next image to the stitched series. Figure 2.2 illustrates a possible process that stitches in column direction first and later assembles those images row by row. As the region of interest (ROI) of the inspected specimen might be unaligned to the acquired images, e.g. the specimen's ROI might have a certain bias. Great care is needed to crop the resulting stitched images to make a useful composition row by row in the second step. In practice, that means a consecutive image adds not only new content in either column or row direction but also a combination of both, this misalignment needs to be compensated. In the above example a cross-correlation coefficient was used to estimate this compensation.

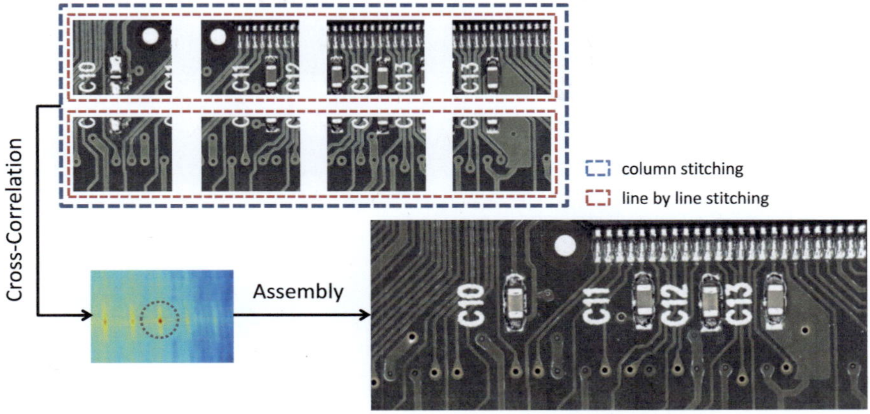

Figure 2.2: Input images are assembled together by stitching them column wise first and afterwards combining the resulting rows.

2.3 Combining established camera inspection techniques with microscope measurement

In this example, industrial camera inspection is combined with microscope inspection, both setups are therefore integrated into an industrial QA process. The industrial camera is used to acquire an overview image and performing a completeness check by applying a correlation based pattern matching method as shown in equation (2.1). A pattern represented by $w(x, y)$ is moved over an image $f(x, y)$ while constantly evaluating the before mentioned cross correlation coefficient $\gamma(x, y)$. $\bar{f}$ and $\bar{w}$ represent the average value of f and w depending on the pattern dimensions and position. The position of the maximum value γ_{max} corresponds to the best matching location $p_{\gamma_{max}} = (x_{max}, y_{max})$:

$$\gamma(x,y) = \frac{\sum_s \sum_t [w(s,t) - \bar{w}] \sum_s \sum_t \left[f(x+s, y+t) - \bar{f}(x+s, y+t)\right]}{\sqrt{\sum_s \sum_t [w(s,t) - \bar{w}]^2 \sum_s \sum_t \left[f(x+s, y+t) - \bar{f}(x+s, y+t)\right]^2}} \quad (2.1)$$

$$\gamma_{max} = \max_{x,y} \gamma(x,y)$$

$$p_{\gamma_{max}} = \arg\max_{x,y} \gamma(x,y)$$

γ_{max} itself can be used as a quality criterion for the matching result, which can be utilized for a completeness check. If the resulting value γ_{max} is less than a

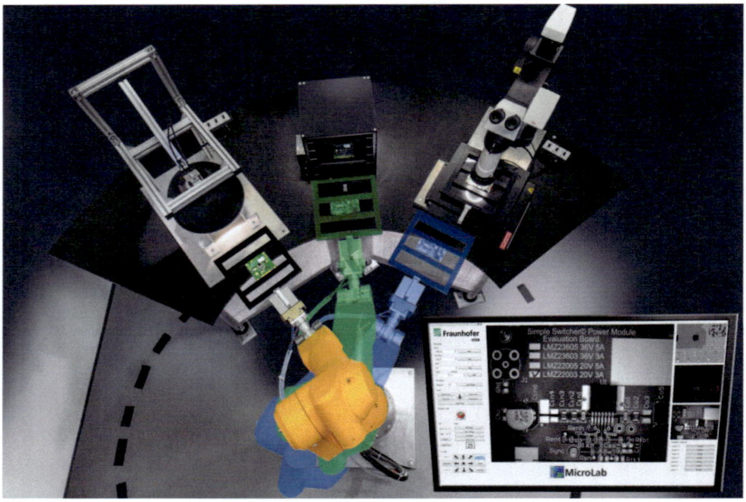

Figure 2.3: Example Setup: An industrial robot (center) cares for the specimen handling between industrial camera (left), specimen buffer (middle) and microscope (right).

certain threshold, it is assumed, that the pattern is missing on the acquired overview image [GW08].

The hardware setup includes an industrial robot which features six axis and is additionally equipped with a pneumatic parallel gripper attached to its 6th axis. This robot is used for transporting the technical goods between an industrial camera and a motorized stage attached to a microscope. Figure 2.3 shows this experimental setup, which consists of the industrial robot, an industrial camera, the microscope and a magazine which simulates a production buffer.

The industrial QA process is simulated by running an endless loop of the following tasks:

- The industrial robot takes a sample s_i out of the magazine and puts it under the industrial camera inspection system
- The industrial camera acquires an overview image to perform a completeness check. Coordinates of the ROI are stored and forwarded to the controller of the global inspection system.
- The robot transfers the specimen to the microscope, which is then performing a detailed analysis of the previously selected regions

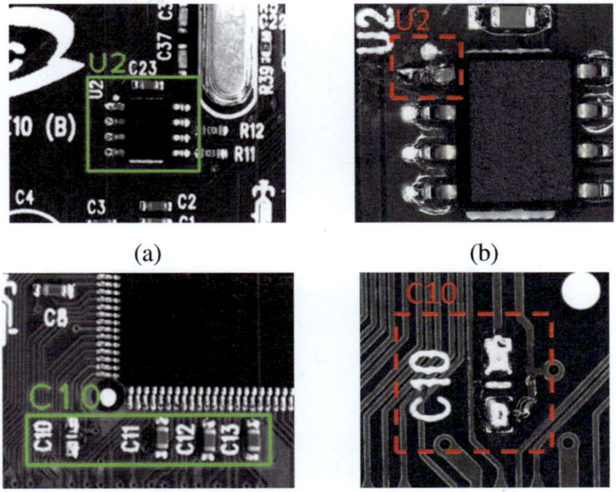

(a) (b)

(c) (d)

Figure 2.4: Camera inspection is unable to detect the defects in (a) and (c), while the microscopy inspection with its larger lateral resolution can detect those easily (b) and in the detail of *C10* in (d).

- The specimen is transferred back into the magazine and the next sample s_{i+1} is processed

For a detailed analysis of the previously computed ROIs, the industrial camera's overview image needs to be calibrated to the positioning stage of the microscope. A solution by estimating an affine transformation is shown in [FSB15]. Figure 2.4 illustrates that the camera inspection can only be used as an indicator when classifying in detail. Especially, smaller chips, represented by too few pixels are misidentified. It is shown though that an existing camera inspection system can be extended by a microscope inspection system.

3 Model based 3D estimation of dirt particles

The methods described in the previous section are used to create the basis for a model based estimation of 2D and later 3D dirt particles by implementing requirements VDA 19 Part 2 recommends [dA14]. VDA 19 Part 2 is a nonbinding recommendation concerning the technical cleanliness of functional relevant parts

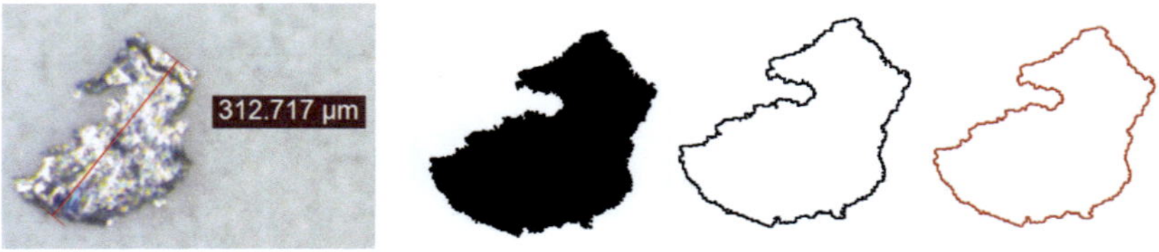

(a) (b) (c) (d)

Figure 3.1: Microscope image of a dirt particle (a) and its segmentation from background (b). The outline was produced with an edge detector (c). That result was pruned to yield slim borders (d).

in automobile industry. Among others, the maximum lateral distance (diameter) of a particle and the particle's height is of important value. The depth map introduced in section 2.1 will be used to estimate an average height of such a particle. Additionally the fourier-descriptors are used to build a model for the particle's outline, which is needed to determine the region covered by that particle.

3.1 Using fourier descriptors to describe the base area of a particle

The algorithm to extract the outline of such a particle consists of three steps:

1. Segmentation of the particle from the background 3.1(b).
2. Estimation of the outline 3.1(c).
3. Pruning of the outline to get an outline of 1px width 3.1(d).

In our application the first step is simple, because the particle background is in general of very bright color value and therefore the particles are shaping up nicely. A threshold applied on the grayscale image is sufficient to complete this task. The boundary is estimated with an edge detector like Sobel, Prewitt, Hewitt or others [GW08]. The last step is necessary to compute an outline that is unambiguous for later comparison with other particles and also minimal concerning the contour.

The outline can be represented by a list of points, starting with a user defined first point. Algorithms in literature often use the centroid of an outline in order to estimate the Centroid Contour Distance Curve (CCDC) [Pav78]. After selecting the starting point, the next point p_i on the outline with a minimal distance to the

(a) (b) (c) (d) (e)

Figure 3.2: Inverse transformation with varying number of p coefficients used. From left to right: $p = 2, 10, 20, 50$.

previous point p_{i-1} is processed. This action is repeated until all points p_j on the boundary have been added to the point sequence $s(k) = [x(k), y(k)]$, $k = 0, 1, 2, \ldots, K-1$. Each point can now be treated as a complex number with $s(k) = x(k) + iy(k)$, which enables us to describe those 2D points in 1D space [GW08]. The complex fourier descriptors $a(u)$ are computed by:

$$a(u) = \sum_{k=0}^{K-1} s(k) \exp\left(\frac{-i2\pi uk}{K}\right).$$

$s(k)$ can be restored by applying the inverse fourier transform as follows:

$$s(k) = \frac{1}{K} \sum_{u=0}^{K-1} a(u) \exp\left(\frac{i2\pi uk}{K}\right).$$

The number of coefficients can be reduced when computing the inverse fourier transformation, which cuts higher frequencies and while keeping the lower descriptors a more global shape of the original boundary is yielded:

$$\hat{s}(k) = \frac{1}{P} \sum_{u=0}^{P-1} a(u) \exp\left(\frac{i2\pi uk}{P}\right), P \leq K. \tag{3.1}$$

Furthermore, the fourier descriptor holds the possibility to describe an outline in a compact form. When reducing the number of descriptors as seen in equation (3.1), a more general shape of the outline is deduced after the inverse transformation was applied, as shown in figure (3.2). This is beneficial, not only for a generalization, but also when building a classifier to discriminate several classes of particles.

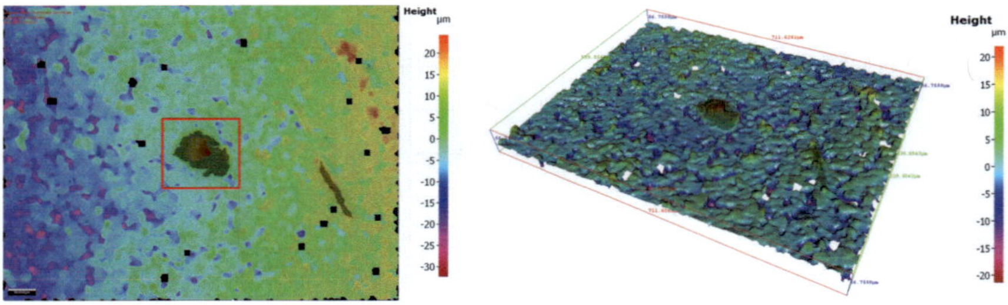

(a) (b)

Figure 3.3: 3D Reconstruction with an Alicona InfinitFocus measurement sensor. 2D image (a) and 3D reconstruction (b).

3.2 Combining lateral information with estimated height information

With the help of a depth map, as seen in section 2.1 a relative height value, which is representing the amount the z-axis was moved, for every pixel of the original specimen is given. The outline description by fourier descriptors serves to construct a bitmask, which is multiplied by the depth map. The result is used to compute the volume V_p of a particle p by iterating over the masked depth map M with the lateral dimensions $w \times h$. As the area A of a squared shaped pixel is already known from the microscope's internal calibration, the computation consists of the following block shaped discrete summation steps, when assuming convex and completely filled particles:

$$V_p(w, h) = A \cdot \sum_{i=0}^{h} \sum_{j=0}^{w} M(i, j).$$

This 2.5D information can also be obtained from state of the art 3D sensors as seen in figure 3.3. In order to find a robust model when optimizing the chosen focus measurement, those established sensors can be used as a ground-truth to support the introduced model. This approach can be seen as multi-sensor fusion. In practice it is difficult to measure the very same spot with two different microscopes, because the specimen handling needs to be exact within the range of a few micrometers. The ground-truth is also of high value when too few height measurements of a given particle exist, as it yields the opportunity to introduce a model based height estimation approach.

4 Conclusion

This technical report motivated specific scenarios when widespread image acquisition sensors, represented by industrial cameras, need to be enhanced with microscopy. Quality Assurance is an important task in nowadays production cycles. Especially, the first part of this report presents methods, already known from industrial image processing, which can be transferred to a microscopic level. The second part of this paper describes a simple model, which is used to reconstruct 3D information out of 2D sensor data on the one hand and also to estimate the volume of dirt particles within the background of VDA 19. Further evaluation steps include the comparison of those results with ground-truth measurements acquired by widely accepted sensors, like whitelight interferometers or confocal microscopes.

Bibliography

[dA14] Verband der Automobilindustrie. *VDA Band 19 Prüfung der Technischen Sauberkeit - Partikelverunreinigung funktionsrelevanter Automobilteile*, 2014.

[FKB14] Peter Frühberger, Edmund Klaus, and Jürgen Beyerer. Microscopic analysis using gaze-based interaction. volume 154 of *Springer Proceedings in Physics*, 2014.

[FSB15] Peter Frühberger, Thomas Stephan, and Jürgen Beyerer. Integrating microscopic analysis into existing quality assurance processes. volume 154 of *Springer Proceedings in Physics*, 2015.

[GW08] Rafael C. Gonzalez and Richard E. Woods. *Digital Image Processing*. Pearson International Edition, 3 edition, 2008.

[Pav78] Theodosios Pavlidis. Review of algorithms for shape analysis. *Computer Graphics and Image Processing*, 7:243–258, 1978.

Fast Face Recognition by Using an Inverted Index

Christian Herrmann

Vision and Fusion Laboratory
Institute for Anthropomatics
Karlsruhe Institute of Technology (KIT), Germany
christian.herrmann@kit.edu

Technical Report IES-2014-02

Abstract: This report addresses the task of searching for faces in large video datasets. Despite vast progress in the field, face recognition remains a challenge for uncontrolled large scale applications like searching for persons in surveillance footage or internet videos. While current productive systems focus on the best shot approach, where only one representative frame from a given face track is selected, thus sacrificing recognition performance, systems achieving state-of-the-art recognition performance, like the recently published DeepFace [TYRW14], ignore recognition speed, which makes them impractical for large scale applications. We suggest a set of measures to address the problem. First, considering the feature location allows collecting the extracted features in according sets. Secondly, the inverted index approach, which became popular in the area of image retrieval, is applied to these feature sets. A face track is thus described by a set of local indexed visual words which enables a fast search. In this way, all information from a face track is collected which allows better recognition performance than best shot approaches and the inverted index permits constantly high recognition speeds. Evaluation on a dataset of several thousand videos shows the validity of the proposed approach.

1 Introduction

Besides the obviously vast collections of video portals like YouTube, large amounts of video footage are also present in surveillance scenarios or the increasing number of TV-channels. Finding specific persons in the data is a still existing challenge. For example, in the context of forensic analysis of surveillance footage, a typical challenge is to find all appearances of a specific person, probably a criminal, in the given data for crime reconstruction. Another example might be to find all YouTube videos containing a specific celebrity. While the latter situation offers further clues like video tags or titles, the former situation requires a solely image based analysis. In this contribution, we focus on a pure video based solution by analyzing the video content, thus covering all scenarios. The easiest way to identify persons in video data is by their face. The first necessary steps before face recognition are face detection, alignment and tracking. Because this is a whole field of research itself, we assume that a solution to these steps is available. The focus lies on comparing and matching the extracted face tracks to a given query.

A high recognition speed combined with a decent recognition performance is achieved by a set of measures. First, collecting all local image features of a face track in a single feature set allows the application of classical image retrieval methods. Secondly, the recognition accuracy is enhanced by using the location of the image features and asserting that only features from the same location will be compared. Thirdly, the inverted index approach, which became popular in the area of image retrieval, is applied to that feature set. A face track is thus described by a set of indexed visual words and for each word a reference to this track is stored in the database index. Searching the database for a given person requires only an index lookup for the respective visual words of the face track. Because the index data structure can be pre-computed for database lookups, query time is low. Evaluation on two public datasets containing several thousand videos shows the validity of the proposed approach. This work addresses two areas of video face recognition:

Face track description. The usual way to build a face track descriptor from video data is a two step strategy. In the first step, each frame is represented by a frame descriptor. There is a large variety of descriptors available from image based face recognition: gray scale intensity, Eigenfaces [TP91], Fisherfaces [BHK97], LBP [AHP06], Gabor [ZJN07] to name only a few. In the second step, a track descriptor is derived from the sequence of frame descriptors, for example by taking the mean over all frames on image [JB08], feature [HLT14, OWS13] or decision level [TBS12, WL13]. Further options include modeling the space of the frames by a linear model [CT10, YFM98], a manifold [AC09b, LHYK03] or performing a pairwise comparison of all [WHM11], randomly selected [TYRW14] or the best-shot [WHM11] frame descriptors and searching for the closest match. Pairwise comparison takes considerable time for larger numbers of involved frames, influenced by track length and percentage of selected frames. In the case of the currently best performing video based face recognition algorithm DeepFace [TYRW14], which compares randomly sampled frames, simulations with the reported feature dimensions and frame numbers indicate matching speeds of only 500 track to track comparisons per second, which is insufficient for large scale applications. Promising methods with respect to matching speed are the ones using small track descriptors and fast comparison strategies. Namely these are the mutual subspace method (MSM) [YFM98] and the best-shot approach. Especially the best-shot approach where the best frame according to some criterion (e.g. most frontal pose or least blurred), is used to represent the whole track, is widely used in time critical applications.

Instead of the frame based strategy, we follow the suggestions of a few recently proposed approaches, which use a local feature based representation [LHL+13, PSVZ14]. Local features are collected over all frames and put together into one feature set. We propose to use this feature set as the base of a bag of visual words descriptor with an inverted index [SZ03], which enables the construction of large databases and performing fast queries. One advantage of the bag of visual words descriptor is its independence of the track length, making comparison tasks independent thereof.

Spatial feature information. Augmenting the local features by the respective image coordinates proved useful for face recognition tasks [LHL+13, PSVZ14]. In the previous contributions, augmentation is performed by concatenation of the feature vector and the 2D image coordinate vector. Instead of a concatenation, we propose a different way to use spatial information, constructing a separate feature set for each of a few fixed feature locations.

2 Frame features

As argued before, instead of using descriptors based on whole frames, a different strategy is applied as illustrated by figure 2.1. For comparison, the conventional frame based method is shown at the top, which uses a face descriptor d_j for each frame j, built by the concatenation of several local features vectors $f_{i,j}$, where i denotes the feature location. The final track descriptor is derived from the sequence $(d_1, \dots, d_n)$ of all n frame descriptors. The feature based track description is shown at the bottom. In this case the face descriptor d'_j is only a mathematical utility, but has no meaning by itself. Basically, all local features $f_{i,j}$ are combined to one feature set, which is used as track descriptor t'. There are three advantages for this method: First, the dimension D' of the vectors in t' is lower than that of the vectors in t, because t' consists of feature vectors $f_{i,j}$ instead of frame descriptors d. Technically speaking, $D = k^2 \cdot D'$ when splitting each face image into a grid of $k \times k$ regions. Thus, further processing can be performed faster, because basically all matching approaches scale at least linearly with D'. Secondly, this representation ignores temporal information. While loosing information is generally a bad idea, it is the opposite in this case, because temporal information includes no clues

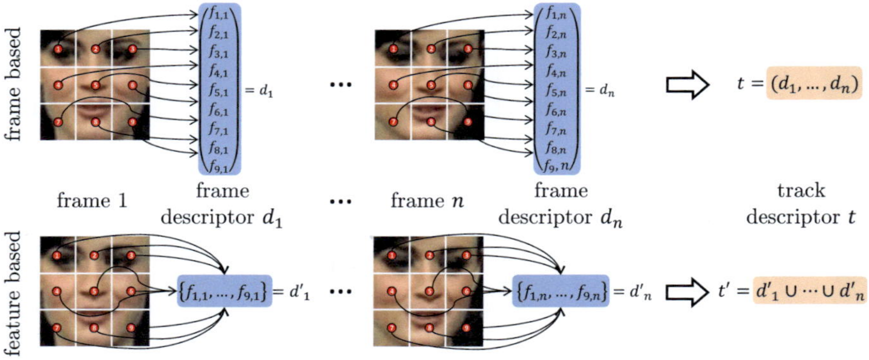

Figure 2.1: Illustration of the conventional frame based track description method (top) and the applied feature set based one (bottom). Local features are denoted by $f_{i,j}$.

about a persons identity. For example, the fact that the head rotates in the face track includes no information about who is rotating his head. Thirdly, the feature based representation is widely used in object or image retrieval tasks, which means according approaches can be applied to face retrieval too.

We employ local binary patterns (LBP) [AHP06] as local features and combine several scales by summation of the LBP histograms [Her13] in each local region. Each face image is split into a grid of $k \times k$ regions, where the region center denotes the location of the local feature. The LBP histogram is built over all LBP patterns inside of a local region. All in all, the proposed strategy results in a set S of $L = k^2 n$ local features for a track with n frames.

3 Bag of words and inverted index

Generally speaking, a retrieval scenario involves a database of N objects and a query object Q. The task is to find all matching objects to the query object in the database. When targeting large scale retrieval applications, the inverted index method is a well-known approach. Basically, this includes three steps, shown also by figure 3.1:

Description of objects with visual words. Each object, in our case each face track, is described by a set of predefined visual words. Possible visual words are defined by a codebook (dictionary) which is constructed by clustering all

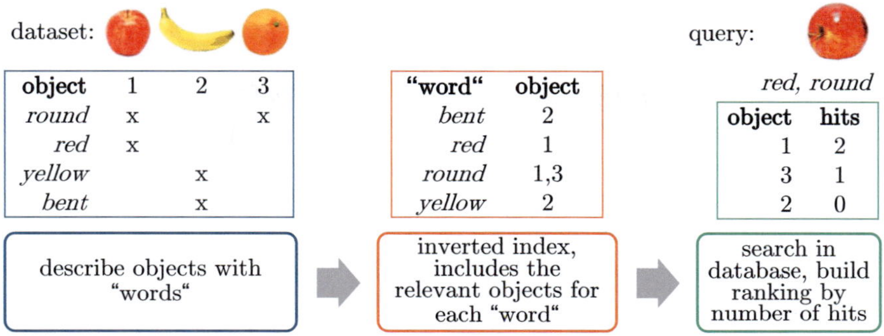

Figure 3.1: Illustration of the inverted index approach with a basic example using images of fruit instead of face tracks and regular words instead of visual ones.

the object features of the database in K classes and using the cluster centers $C_1, \ldots, C_K$ as visual words. In this way, the codebook consists of domain specific visual words. For each object, the feature set S from the previous section is computed and the matching words are found by assigning each feature to the nearest visual word. The set of occurring words represents the object.

Building an inverted index for the whole database of objects. To avoid linear search for the best matches in the database, an inverted index is used. This means an index with the visual words from the codebook is constructed and for each visual word a list of objects including this word is maintained.

Database query by indexed search for the visual words of the query object. Performing a search for a query object first requires to find the visual words for the query object. Then, for each visual word of the query object the matching database objects are looked up in the index. Finally, counting the number of hits for the matching database objects results in a ranking. Note that in large scale applications it is common that a significant part of the database objects has no hits at all.

Using the inverted index strategy without adaptation has a serious drawback. Because all visual features are put together into a single feature set, their location in the face is lost. While this behavior is usually desired in image retrieval, because it guarantees invariance to rotation, scaling and shifting, it is counterproductive in face retrieval. Face detections are always aligned, thus they have a known and fixed rotation, scaling and are shifted equally. In this way, the feature location is meaningful in contradiction to image retrieval and it can be used to improve the results. Because the nose is always in the middle, eyes at the top, mouth at the

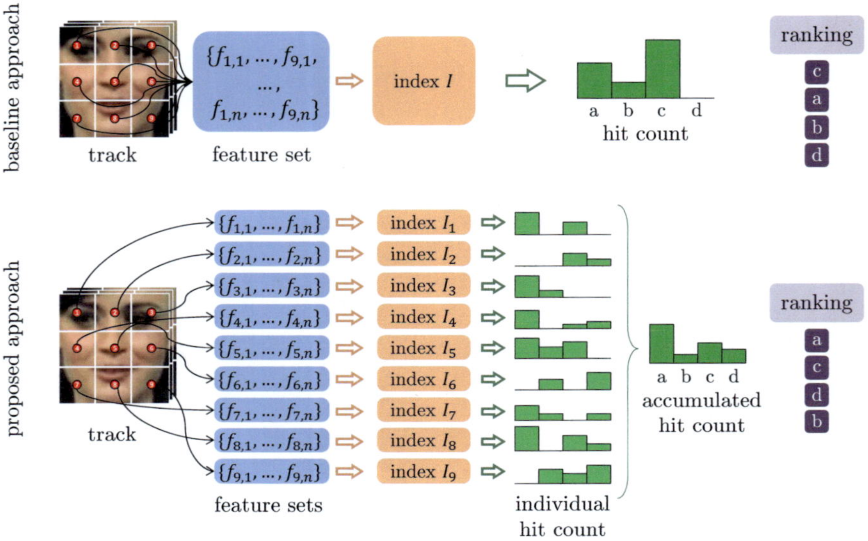

Figure 3.2: Comparison of basic (top) and proposed (bottom) strategy. Illustration shows a query process for a small sample database whose face tracks are called a, b, c and d.

bottom and so on, comparing features from different locations is unnecessary. It has no meaning if the nose of one person shows the same feature as the eye of another one. Thus, instead of using one single index for all features, we suggest to use separate local indices as shown by figure 3.2 at the bottom. Each feature location in the grid, is handled individually and results are combined at the end by accumulating the hit counts from the different index searches.

Practical issues: The inverted index method includes to basic problems where fast algorithms are necessary. First, the clustering of a large dataset to build the index and secondly, the nearest neighbor search to assign the corresponding visual word to a feature. The VLFeat library [VF08] is used in both cases because it uses efficient algorithms based on KD-trees.

4 Experiments

To show the benefits of the proposed method, evaluation is performed on the largest publicly available datasets YouTube Faces Database (YTF) [WHM11] and Face in Action Database (FiA) [GLLC05]. While YTF is an in the wild dataset with 3,425 face videos originating from YouTube containing celebrities, FiA data was recorded in the lab in a controlled environment with fixed camera positions and predefined head movements resulting in 3,110 face videos (only indoor sequences are used).

4.1 Experimental setup

The retrieval evaluation protocol is a 10 fold strategy: the dataset is divided into 10 splits and each one will be used one after another as query split, while the remaining 9 splits build the database. Each track in a query split is used to query the database, which results, over all 10 splits, in M queries, where M is the dataset size.

Performance is measured by the average precision a for each query and overall given by the mean average precision map. The average precision measures a the quality of the resulting ranking for a query by the recall r and precision p. The recall $r = \frac{TP}{TP+FN}$ denotes the percentage of the number of retrieved correct matches TP and the number of all possible correct matches $TP + FN$ in a database. TP, FP and FN are notations from classification tasks, meaning *true positives*, *false positives* and *false negatives*. In this way, the precision $p = \frac{TP}{TP+FP}$ denotes the ratio of correct hits in the returned query. Let $r(k)$ denote the recall for retrieval results consisting of the ranks 1 to k and $p(k)$ the respective precision. Then the average precision for one ranking is given by $a = \sum_{k=1}^{K} \Delta r(k) \cdot p(k)$, which is a weighted average of the precision over all ranks. Finally, the mean average precision is the mean over all queries: $map = \frac{1}{M} \sum_{m=1}^{M} a_m$. The map ranges between 0 and 1, where a value of 1 signals a perfect result with all the correct matches at the top of the ranking.

Significant pairwise differences between measured values are determined by a randomization test [SAC07], using an α-level of 0.05, which corresponds to a confidence of about 2 standard deviations. In comparison to simply giving the mean and standard deviation, it has the advantage to statistically exploit the large number of queries which are performed in this experimental setup. Thus, it is more accurate in showing significant differences between retrieval algorithms.

In contrast to a simple verification protocol, where 10-fold cross-validation provides only a shallow statistical base for proving significant differences between approaches, the retrieval protocol offers M samples. In consequence, significant pairwise differences between measured values are determined by a randomization test [SAC07], using an α-level of 0.05, which corresponds to a confidence of about 2 standard deviations. In comparison to reporting only the mean and standard deviation, it has the advantage to statistically exploit the large number of

Case	Algorithm	$\bar{K}$	Feature	Local indices	map	rand. test	t_q in s	t_m in s
1	inv. index	64000	LBP	no	0.013		0.062	$4.50 \cdot 10^3$
2	inv. index	64000	LBP	yes	**0.052**	1	0.050	$0.51 \cdot 10^3$
3	inv. index	64000	Intensity	yes	0.046	5	0.037	$0.86 \cdot 10^3$
4	inv. index	64000	LBP	yes	**0.052**	3,5	0.050	$0.51 \cdot 10^3$
5	inv. index	64000	LDP	yes	0.022		0.087	$0.52 \cdot 10^3$
6	inv. index	64000	LBP	yes	0.052		0.050	$0.51 \cdot 10^3$
7	inv. index	128000	LBP	yes	0.058	6	0.067	$0.91 \cdot 10^3$
8	inv. index	256000	LBP	yes	0.061	6,7	0.116	$1.78 \cdot 10^3$
9	inv. index	512000	LBP	yes	**0.067**	6,7,8	0.123	$3.66 \cdot 10^3$

Table 4.1: Evaluation of different features and parameters. Randomization test column denotes case numbers which yielded significantly worse results.

queries which are performed in this experimental setup. Thus, it is more accurate in showing significant differences between retrieval algorithms.

4.2 Parameters

In the first set of experiments, parameter variations for the proposed method are evaluated on the YTF dataset and results are shown in table 4.1. Besides the map and the respective randomization tests, the mean time t_q for one query and the database construction time t_m are given.

Local indices. Using a separate local index for each spatial feature location enhances the retrieval results significantly (case 2). Thus, mixing together different features causes confusion in the recognition process and the separation solves this issue. For fair comparison between the baseline global inverted index and the local inverted indices, the sum $\bar{K}$ of the respective dictionary sizes is given. For the baseline (case 1) this means $\bar{K} = K$ is the size of the single dictionary, while in the case of local indices each dictionary has the size of $K = \frac{\bar{K}}{k^2}$, where k^2 is the number of local regions as in section 2.

Feature. Comparison to different features, namely raw pixel intensities (case 4) and local directional patterns (LDP) [JKC10], indicates that the proposed usage of LBP from section 2 is justified. $k = 4$ local regions are used in all cases because it has proved to be the best subdivision for resolutions on this level [Her13].

Index size. Retrieval results get better with an increasing index size (cases 6-9). Further increases are prevented by the limited memory of our test system. Thus for the further experiments in the next section we use the setting from case 9.

4.3 Comparison

As already stated in the introduction, only few face recognition approaches are capable of fast matching for large scale face retrieval. Thus the number of possible baseline approaches remains limited for comparison. Namely, we employ MSM, pairwise-frame matching (NN) and best-shot on the same LBP features. The final results are shown in table 4.2 for evaluation on YTF, FiA and the combination of both datasets. Although, NN shows clearly the highest map, it requires heavy computational work which is impractical for real applications. MSM and best-shot decrease the mean query time t_q significantly, however, both are a trade-off between speed and accuracy. The proposed inverted index method manages to break this trade-off in certain limits. While results for YTF fall in between the results of the best-shot and MSM method, they are significantly better for FiA. Comparing the results of the best-shot method with the inverted index results from the previous section (table 4.1, case 7) indicates that the proposed method has a better recognition performance per time ratio than the best-shot method. Finally, the combination of both datasets clearly shows the advantage of the inverted index method: the mean query times remains constant and independent of database size, thus making it the fastest retrieval method for larger datasets. The reason is the avoidance of a linear search in the database. Thus, increasing the database size by a combination of both datasets has only minor influences on the query time for the inverted index compared to the baseline approaches, where the query time roughly doubles with the doubled dataset size.

5 Conclusion

A face retrieval method based on local features and an inverted index is proposed. By using a separate local index for each spatial feature location instead of only one global index, the recognition accuracy for the inverted index approach can be increased significantly. In this way, the widely used best-shot method is outperformed while showing smaller query times for large scale problems. The key benefit of the proposed system is that its query time is independent of the database size, which promises an increasing advance with growing datasets.

No.	Method	*map* YTF	*map* FiA	*map* comb.	query time t_q in s YTF	query time t_q in s FiA	query time t_q in s comb.
1	NN	0.145^2	0.351^4	0.255^4	12.31	10.37	30.51
2	MSM	0.084^4	0.237^3	0.170^3	0.281	0.150	0.428
3	best shot	0.056	0.147	0.103	0.074	0.069	0.134
4	inv. index	0.067^3	0.297^2	0.183^2	0.123	0.103	0.114

Table 4.2: Evaluation results on YTF and FiA public datasets, as well as a combination of both. Superscripts indicate results of randomization test: a method is significantly better than the one indicated by the superscript, including every worse one.

Bibliography

[AC09b] O. Arandjelović and R. Cipolla. A pose-wise linear illumination manifold model for face recognition using video. *Computer Vision and Image Understanding*, 113(1):113–125, 2009.

[AHP06] Timo Ahonen, Abdenour Hadid, and Matti Pietikainen. Face Description with Local Binary Patterns: Application to Face Recognition. *Pattern Analysis and Machine Intelligence*, 28(12):2037–2041, 2006.

[BHK97] P.N. Belhumeur, J.P. Hespanha, and D.J. Kriegman. Eigenfaces vs. Fisherfaces: Recognition Using Class Specific Linear Projection. *IEEE Transactions on Pattern Analysis and Machine Intelligence*, 19(7):711–720, 1997.

[CT10] H. Cevikalp and B. Triggs. Face recognition based on image sets. In *Computer Vision and Pattern Recognition*, 2010.

[GLLC05] R. Goh, L. Liu, X. Liu, and T. Chen. The CMU Face In Action (FIA) Database. *Analysis and Modelling of Faces and Gestures*, pages 255–263, 2005.

[Her13] Christian Herrmann. Extending a local matching face recognition approach to low-resolution video. In *Advanced Video and Signal Based Surveillance*, 2013.

[HLT14] Junlin Hu, Jiwen Lu, and Yap-Peng Tan. Discriminative deep metric learning for face verification in the wild. In *Computer Vision and Pattern Recognition*, pages 1875–1882, 2014.

[JB08] Rob Jenkins and AM Burton. 100% Accuracy In Automatic Face Recognition. *Science*, 319(5862):435–435, 2008.

[JKC10] Taskeed Jabid, Md Hasanul Kabir, and Oksam Chae. Local directional pattern (LDP) for face recognition. In *Consumer Electronics*, pages 329–330, 2010.

[LHL+13] Haoxiang Li, Gang Hua, Zhe Lin, Jonathan Brandt, and Jianchao Yang. Probabilistic elastic matching for pose variant face verification. In *Computer Vision and Pattern Recognition*, 2013.

[LHYK03] K.C. Lee, J. Ho, M.H. Yang, and D. Kriegman. Video-Based Face Recognition Using Probabilistic Appearance Manifolds. *Computer Vision and Pattern Recognition*, 1:313–320, 2003.

[OWS13] Enrique G Ortiz, Alan Wright, and Mubarak Shah. Face recognition in movie trailers via mean sequence sparse representation-based classification. In *Computer Vision and Pattern Recognition*, 2013.

[PSVZ14] Omkar M Parkhi, Karen Simonyan, Andrea Vedaldi, and Andrew Zisserman. A Compact and Discriminative Face Track Descriptor. In *Computer Vision and Pattern Recognition*, 2014.

[SAC07] Mark D Smucker, James Allan, and Ben Carterette. A comparison of statistical significance tests for information retrieval evaluation. In *Information and Knowledge Management*, 2007.

[SZ03] Josef Sivic and Andrew Zisserman. Video Google: A text retrieval approach to object matching in videos. In *International Conference on Computer Vision*, pages 1470–1477, 2003.

[TBS12] Makarand Tapaswi, M Bäuml, and Rainer Stiefelhagen. "Knock! Knock! Who is it?" probabilistic person identification in TV-series. In *Computer Vision and Pattern Recognition*, pages 2658–2665, 2012.

[TP91] M. Turk and A. Pentland. Eigenfaces for Recognition. *Journal of Cognitive Neuroscience*, 3(1):71–86, 1991.

[TYRW14] Yaniv Taigman, Ming Yang, Marc'Aurelio Ranzato, and Lior Wolf. Deepface: Closing the gap to human-level performance in face verification. In *Computer Vision and Pattern Recognition*, pages 1701–1708, 2014.

[VF08] A. Vedaldi and B. Fulkerson. VLFeat: An Open and Portable Library of Computer Vision Algorithms. `http://www.vlfeat.org/`, 2008.

[WHM11] L. Wolf, T. Hassner, and I. Maoz. Face recognition in unconstrained videos with matched background similarity. In *Computer Vision and Pattern Recognition*, 2011.

[WL13] Lior Wolf and Noga Levy. The svm-minus similarity score for video face recognition. In *Computer Vision and Pattern Recognition*, 2013.

[YFM98] O. Yamaguchi, K. Fukui, and K. Maeda. Face Recognition Using Temporal Image Sequence. In *Automatic Face and Gesture Recognition*, 1998.

[ZJN07] Jie Zou, Qiang Ji, and George Nagy. A Comparative Study of Local Matching Approach for Face Recognition. *IEEE Transactions on Image Processing*, 16(10):2617–2628, 2007.

Wavelet-based Methods for Classification of Surface Measurement Data

Tan-Toan Le

Institute for Applied Research
Pforzheim University, Germany
tan-toan.le@hs-pforzheim.de

Technical Report IES-2014-03

Abstract: In this work various applications of wavelet filter banks for evaluation of different classification problems in image processing are presented. For the evaluation a new method for designing bi-orthogonal wavelet-filter-banks is introduced. By this method the most dominant stretchings of all defects from the same class are first determined. After that the filter bank is designed to have the same lengths as these stretchings. On the other hand the filter is also designed to match the curve shape of the defect. In this way the bi-orthogonal wavelet filter bank can better match the defects which therefore enhances classification rate. A comparison with classification results based on other standard wavelet families as well as non-wavelet methods was also performed.

1 Introduction

The disadvantage of using classical wavelet families in image processing is that these wavelet families were not optimized exactly for this image processing problem and therefore the classification or detection results may fall short of expectations. As a solution for this problem two different optimization methods for designing wavelet filter bank are introduced in this paper. The first method optimizes an M-channel bi-orthogonal wavelet filter bank (*MCFB*) on the profile of the defect. One of the limitations of traditional wavelet filter banks is that the sampling factors are integers and this restricts the adaptation of filter lengths to different feature's stretchings. To overcome this obstacle the wavelet filter banks can be designed to have rational sampling factors, keeping the wavelet properties of the filter bank as well. The second method presented in this paper is the optimization of these rational wavelet filter banks (*RWFB*). For better classification and for improved detection rates the optimized wavelet filter bank must be in possession of two properties: on the one hand it should contain the profile of the feature class as mentioned in the first method, on the other hand it should also match the most dominant stretchings of the feature. To evaluate the designing methods *MCFB* and *RWFB* the data from surface measurement by different image processing problems were applied. These data were acquired in the first case from deflectometry measurement of specular surfaces with the goal to be classified and in the second case from metal surfaces with the contaminations to be detected.

2 Optimization Methods for Wavelet Filter Banks

2.1 M-Channel Optimized Wavelet Filter Banks

The optimization method *MCFB* presented in [Le14] is briefly summarized here. The goal of this optimization is to design an M-channel filter bank $\boldsymbol{h}_t$ ($t = 0, \ldots, M-1$), where the channels $\boldsymbol{h}_t$ are bi-orthogonal to each other and besides that the filter bank should have the characteristic of defect, which need be detected or classified. A one-dimensional profile $\boldsymbol{h}_F$ of the defect to be detected is therefore firstly extracted. The first $(M-1)$ channels of the filter bank are designed to have the same curve as this profile, meanwhile the last channel is constructed to be on one hand as different from the defect profile as possible, on the other hand bi-orthogonal with the other channels. In this way by filtering with the defect, the first $(M-1)$ channels give strong impulse responses.

2.1.1 Optimizing the filter bank channel to match the defect profile

In the first step the object class to be detected on the surface was extracted, so that a typical curve can be presented. Based on this curve, a profile filter $\boldsymbol{h}_F$ could be designed, which has impulse responses with the same course as the defect to represent the defect. The first $(M-1)$ channels of the M-channel filter bank receive the same profile as the filter $\boldsymbol{h}_F$ of the defect classes. The filter $\boldsymbol{h}_{M-1}$ should be bi-orthogonal to other filters in the filter bank as well as different from the object profile. A quality criterion Q is defined as the Euclidean distance between the profile filter $\boldsymbol{h}_F$ of the defect class C_F and the filter to be constructed $\boldsymbol{h}_{M-1}$:

$$Q = \|\boldsymbol{h}_F - \boldsymbol{h}_{M-1}\|^2.$$

By maximizing the quality criterion Q, the filter $\boldsymbol{h}_{M-1}$ will be optimized to be as different from the given defect class as possible.

2.1.2 Bi-orthogonal criteria for filter bank design

For an M-channel filter bank consisting of $(M-1)$ filters $\boldsymbol{h}_t$ $(t = 0, \ldots, M-2)$, a filter $\boldsymbol{h}_{M-1}$, which is bi-orthogonal to all $\boldsymbol{h}_t$, is to be constructed. Using an M-channel filter bank, an analyzed signal will be perfectly reconstructed from its wavelet coefficients, if the determinant $\Delta_P(z)$ of the polyphase-matrix $P(z)$ of the filters $\boldsymbol{h}_t$ $(t = 0, .., M-1)$ consists of only a single term z^{-n_0} [Gre96]. $P(z)$ has the form:

$$P_{ij}(z) = z^{-j} H_{ij}(z^M).$$

Here $H_{ij}(z^M)$ is the j-th polyphase component of the i-th filter [Vet86]. Its determinant $\Delta_P(z)$ can be calculated as:

$$\Delta_P(z) = c_0 z^{-M\frac{M-1}{2}} + \ldots + c_{N-M} z^{-[MN - M\frac{M+1}{2}]}, \tag{2.1}$$

with the constants c_m, $m = 0, \ldots, N-M$. Due to the condition for perfect reconstruction above, all the constants c_j in (2.1) except one need to be set to zero, so that the determinant $\Delta_P(z)$ contains only a single term. The constants c_j are weighted sums of coefficients of the filter $\boldsymbol{h}_{M-1}$ to be constructed:

$$c_j = \sum_{n=0}^{N-1} a_{mn} \boldsymbol{h}_{M-1}(n).$$

The construction of $\boldsymbol{h}_{M-1}$ can thus be considered as optimizing the quality criterion Q under the constraint that the condition for PR is fulfilled. As a linear system, the set of $(N-M)$ equations $c_j \stackrel{!}{=} 0$, which contain the filter coefficients $\boldsymbol{h}_{M-1}(n)$, $(n = 0, \ldots, N-1)$, is optimized with respect to Q. In order to solve this optimization problem a Lagrange function with Lagrange multiplier $\boldsymbol{\lambda}$ is defined as:

$$L(\boldsymbol{h}_{M-1}, \boldsymbol{\lambda}) = \frac{1}{2} Q - \boldsymbol{\lambda}^T [\boldsymbol{A} \boldsymbol{h}_{M-1} - \mathbf{0}].$$

The optimum can be found by solving the derivation equations:

$$\nabla_{\boldsymbol{h}_{M-1}, \boldsymbol{\lambda}} L(\boldsymbol{h}_{M-1}, \boldsymbol{\lambda}) \stackrel{!}{=} 0.$$

This way, we define the coefficients of filter $\boldsymbol{h}_{M-1}$, which are bi-orthogonal to given filters $\boldsymbol{h}_t$ $(t = 0, ..., M-2)$. Using the approach described above, a typical curve of each defect class is at first extracted and then used to create a representative filter. Figure 2.1 shows the impulse response of a dent filter with length 8 as well as its associated bi-orthogonal wavelet filter.

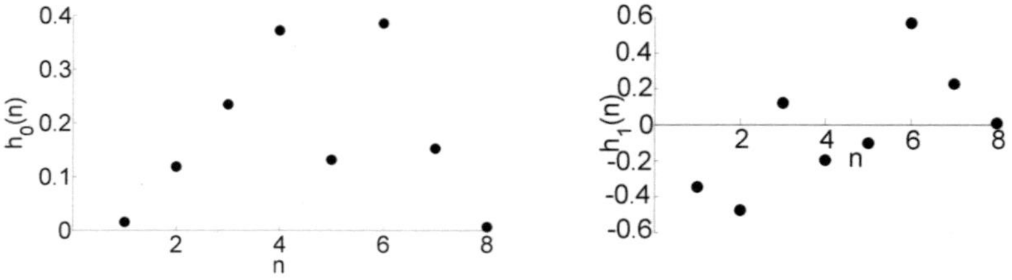

(a) dent filter (b) bi-orthogonal dent filter

Figure 2.1: Impulse responses of a dent filter.

2.2 Rational Wavelet Filter Bank

Due to the rational sampling factor a *RWFB* has the benefit in comparison with other wavelet filter banks that the filter length can be scaled more easily to other desired lengths. In the literature there are many different approaches for designing rational wavelet filter banks [BS09a], [Blu98], ... For our work the method presented by Nguyen [NN13] was chosen, because it allows not only more freedom by choosing sampling factors, it can also construct bi-orthogonal wavelet filter bank, which is important for designing filter coefficients. Figure 2.2 shows a typical bi-orthogonal rational wavelet filter bank designed with this method.

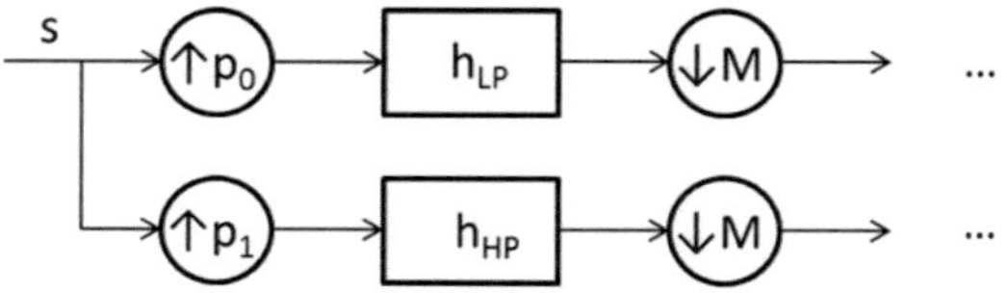

Figure 2.2: A Rational Wavelet Filter Bank

The rational wavelet filter bank can be transformed into an equivalent non-rational uniform filter bank. This transform delivers the possibility to construct a rational wavelet filter bank with perfect reconstruction, which is normally only valid for non-rational uniform filter banks. Mathematically, a wavelet filter bank with perfect reconstruction also allows bi-orthogonality. As long as the z-Transform $H_{LP}(z)$ and $H_{HP}(z)$ of h_{LP} and h_{HP} can be decomposed into:

$$H_{LP}(z) = \sum_{n=0}^{p_0-1} z^{Mn} H_n(z^{p_0}) \text{ and}$$

$$H_{HP}(z) = \sum_{n=0}^{p_1-1} z^{Mn} H_{n+p_0}(z^{p_1}),$$

the rational filter bank is equivalent with an M-channel filter bank $H_0, H_1, ..., H_{p_0+p_1-1}$ [NN13]. This means that, we can transpose a rational wavelet filter bank with sampling factor (p_0/M) and (p_1/M) into a uniform M-channel wavelet filter bank. Based on the uniform filter bank, the conditions for perfect reconstruction, which are also valid for the equivalent rational wavelet filter bank, can be constructed.

2.2.1 Determining dominant defect stretchings

To optimize the rational wavelet filter bank, the most dominant defect stretchings are determined in the first step. Various conventional detecting methods in image processing can be used to determine the defect sizes. Based on these results we can find out, which stretching sizes are most dominant, for example with the help of a size histogram as shown in Figure 2.3. The optimization target is now converted into designing a rational filter bank with filter lengths as the dominant sizes.

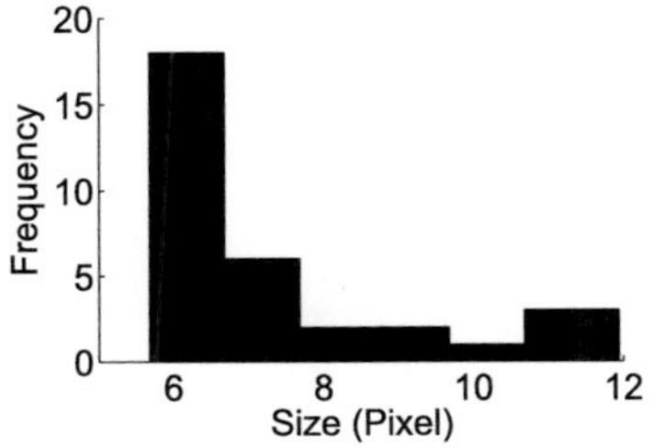

Figure 2.3: Size histogram of class *pimple*

This process can be summarized as in Figure 2.4.

2.2.2 Optimized bi-orthogonal rational Wavelet Filter Banks

The designing of bi-orthogonal rational wavelet filter banks in this work is done in two steps: designing the low pass filter $\boldsymbol{h}_{LP}$ and designing the band pass filter $\boldsymbol{h}_{HP}$ with condition of perfect reconstruction for the filter bank. Before the filter bank is designed, a feature filter $\boldsymbol{h}_F$ is constructed for each defect class as presented in Section 2.1.1.

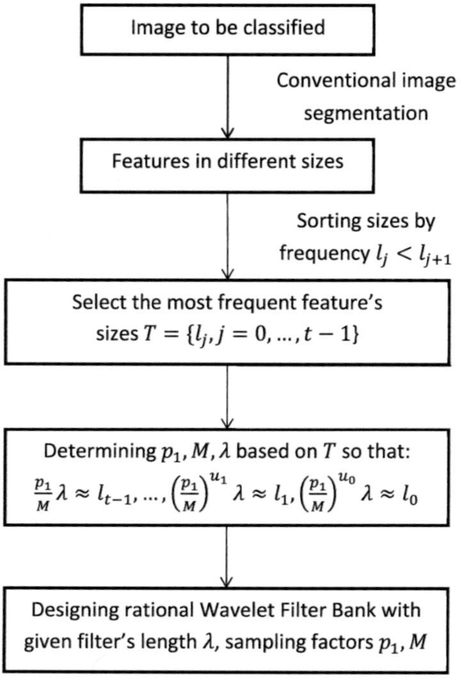

Figure 2.4: Process for determining sampling factors

In the first step the filter $\boldsymbol{h}_{LP}$ is constructed with the help of the optimization function $f_0(\boldsymbol{h}_{LP})$:

$$f_0(\boldsymbol{h}_{LP}) = \boldsymbol{h}_{LP}^T(\boldsymbol{P}_{P_0} + \boldsymbol{P}_{S_0})\boldsymbol{h}_{LP},$$

where $\boldsymbol{P}_{P_0}$ and $\boldsymbol{P}_{S_0}$ are real symmetric positive semi-definite matrices described in [WN99] to optimize the pass band and stop band of $\boldsymbol{h}_{LP}$. The function $f_0(\boldsymbol{h}_{LP})$ can be optimized with the constraint:

$$g_0 : \|\boldsymbol{h}_{LP} - \boldsymbol{h}_F\|^2 > \epsilon_0.$$

The constraint warranties that the filter $\boldsymbol{h}_{LP}$ will own a different curve compared to the feature filter $\boldsymbol{h}_F$.

After this step the coefficients of the filter $\boldsymbol{h}_{LP}$ are given and can be used in the next step, where the filter $\boldsymbol{h}_{HP}$ is optimized. Similar to the optimization function $f_0(\boldsymbol{h}_{LP})$ in the first step, a function $f_1(\boldsymbol{h}_{HP})$ can be constructed as:

$$f_1(\boldsymbol{h}_{HP}) = \boldsymbol{h}_{HP}^T(\boldsymbol{P}_{P_1} + \boldsymbol{P}_{S_1})\boldsymbol{h}_{HP},$$

where $\boldsymbol{P}_{P_1}$ and $\boldsymbol{P}_{S_1}$ are the pass band and stop band of $\boldsymbol{h}_{HP}$ respectively. Moreover $\boldsymbol{h}_{HP}$ should have the same curve as the feature filter $\boldsymbol{h}_F$:

$$g_1 : \|\boldsymbol{h}_{HP} - \boldsymbol{h}_F\|^2 < \epsilon_1.$$

Furthermore the filter $\boldsymbol{h}_{LP}$ should be bi-orthogonal to $\boldsymbol{h}_{HP}$. As described in Section 2.2, it is possible to transform the given rational filter bank into an equivalent uniform M-channel filter and the condition for perfect reconstruction can be built based on this filter bank. The rational wavelet filter bank of $\boldsymbol{h}_{LP}$ and $\boldsymbol{h}_{HP}$ with sampling factors (p_0/M) and (p_1/M) have polyphase components $\boldsymbol{h}_i$ of the M-channel filter bank as:

$$\boldsymbol{h}_i[n] = \begin{cases} \boldsymbol{h}_{LP}[i + np_0] \text{ for } i = 0, ..., p_0 - 1, \\ \boldsymbol{h}_{HP}[i - np_0 + np_1] \text{ for } i = p_0, ..., M - 1. \end{cases} \tag{2.2}$$

Due to the condition for perfect reconstruction in Section 2.1.2, all the constants c_m in (2.1) except one need to be set to zero. c_m consist of coefficients of $\boldsymbol{h}_i$, which are also coefficients of $\boldsymbol{h}_{LP}$ and $\boldsymbol{h}_{HP}$ as in (2.2), and hence can be used as constraints for designing $\boldsymbol{h}_{HP}$. The filter $\boldsymbol{h}_{HP}$ can therefore be optimized by minimizing the function $f_1(\boldsymbol{h}_{HP})$ with the constraints $c_m \stackrel{!}{=} 0$ (for all c_m except one) and g_1.

Together with the sampling factors p_0, p_1 and M found in Section 2.2.1 $\boldsymbol{h}_{LP}$ and $\boldsymbol{h}_{HP}$ build a rational wavelet filter bank as in Figure 2.2, which can be used for analyzing data. Coming back to the example of class *pimple* in Figure 2.3 it can be seen that the three most dominant sizes are 6, 7 and 11. Based on this knowledge and the optimization method in Section 2.2.2 a *RWFB* can be constructed. In Figure 2.5 we can find the result of the optimized filter bank. The left figure shows the optimized pimple filter, while the right one shows the pimple filter after the first transformation with the sampling factor. It's obvious that the right figure still has the same profile as the pimple filter and the filter's length is 11, which is one of the three most dominant sizes.

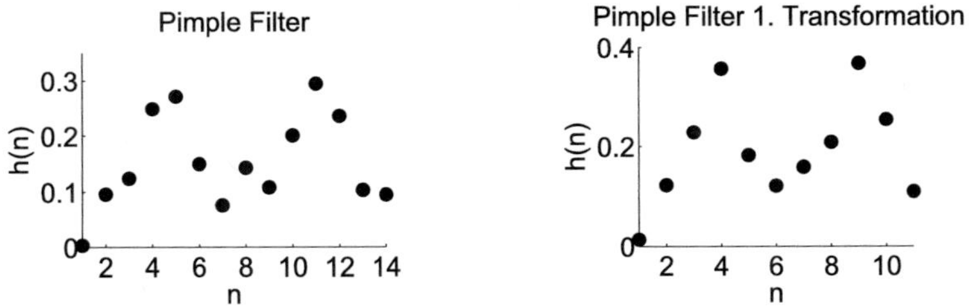

Figure 2.5: Impulse response of pimple matched filter.

3 Applications

After a filter bank was built with the help of optimization methods *MCFB* or *RWFB*, a wavelet packet tree is created, the nodes of this tree can be considered as features for classification purpose. To classify a point (x, y) on the surface S, a set of nodes at the same point $d_k(x, y)$ are chosen to create a feature vector $\boldsymbol{d}$. Based on the idea presented in [ZLGH12], a suitable classifier can be set up. The parameters $\boldsymbol{\mu_i}$ and $\boldsymbol{\sigma_i}$ are considered as mean and standard deviation of each coefficient on the class C_i for all selected nodes in a feature vector $\boldsymbol{d}$. The Bayes' theorem defines the probability p for vector $\boldsymbol{d}$ belonging to class C_i as:

$$p(\boldsymbol{\mu_i}, \boldsymbol{\sigma_i}|\boldsymbol{d}) = \frac{p(\boldsymbol{d}|\boldsymbol{\mu_i}, \boldsymbol{\sigma_i})p(\boldsymbol{\mu_i}, \boldsymbol{\sigma_i})}{p(\boldsymbol{d})}.$$

The distribution of coefficients can be considered as Laplace [ZLGH12]. The likelihood for class C_i can therefore be modelled as the product of a univariate Laplace distribution:

$$p(\boldsymbol{d}|\boldsymbol{\mu_i}, \boldsymbol{\sigma_i}) = \prod_k \frac{1}{\sigma_{i,k}\sqrt{2\pi}} \exp(-\frac{1}{2}\frac{|d_k - \mu_{i,k}|}{\sigma_{i,k}^2}).$$

For each class C_i the parameters $\boldsymbol{\mu_i}$ and $\boldsymbol{\sigma_i}$ are learned with a training set.

The presented designing methods *MCFB* and *RWFB* were applied on different problems in the image processing. The first application should classify the reconstruction measured data from deflectometry. Due to that fact that the reconstructed data are not always available, the method was also applied to registration measured data. As described in [Le14] among the standard wavelet families, the filter bank with *Bi-orthogonal spline wavelets* presented by Cohen [CDF06] seems to be best appropriate for detection and classification purpose of dent and pimple. This wavelet family was used here again as a reference for our optimized wavelet filter banks.

Table 3.1 shows the classification results by applying different methods. Meanwhile by the reconstructed data all methods could deliver relatively good results (about 99% by the class *dent* and 96% by the class *pimple*), by registration measured data the method *RWFB* showed its advantage compared to other methods with up to 99.4% by the class *dent* as well as 92.8% by the class *pimple*. In addition it can also be seen that by *RWFB* the classification rates got better with more number of chosen dominant sizes t.

Another application of the presented methods is the detection of contaminations on metal surfaces. Visible textures on the surface, which are caused by manufacturing

		Accuracy			
		recon. data		**regis. data**	
		dent	*pimple*	*dent*	*pimple*
Matched Filter		98.2%	96.0%	60.3%	66.3%
Bi-orthogonal spline wavelet 3.5		96.8%	94.9%	58.5%	56.2%
Method	**Matched**	*dent*	*pimple*	*dent*	*pimple*
$MCFB$	C_d	99.7%	96.4%	97.9%	80.5%
$MCFB$	C_p	99.7%	96.5%	82.7%	65.1%
$RWFB$	$C_p, t = 1$	99.7%	96.3%	99.0%	81.1%
$RWFB$	$C_p, t = 2$	99.6%	96.3%	99.3%	90.3%
$RWFB$	$C_p, t = 3$	99.3%	95.8%	99.4%	92.8%

Table 3.1: Comparison of the classification accuracy using different wavelet filter banks for our classification method, the classes *dent* C_d and *pimple* C_p.

and which complicate the detection, are present. The contaminations appear on the surfaces in form of black stains as in Figure 3.1. In this case the black stains were considered as feature for the detection purpose. A rational wavelet filter bank was built on this feature to classify data of the metal surfaces. Other methods in image processing were applied for comparison. In Table 3.2 the detection results using the presented wavelet filter bank designing methods *MCFB* and *RWFB* as well as other methods (*Thresholding* and *bi-orthogonal spline wavelet 3.5*) can be found. The detection results show that the filter bank of *RWFB*, with an accuracy up to 96%, worked better than the filter bank of *MCFB* (with 84.5%) and other methods.

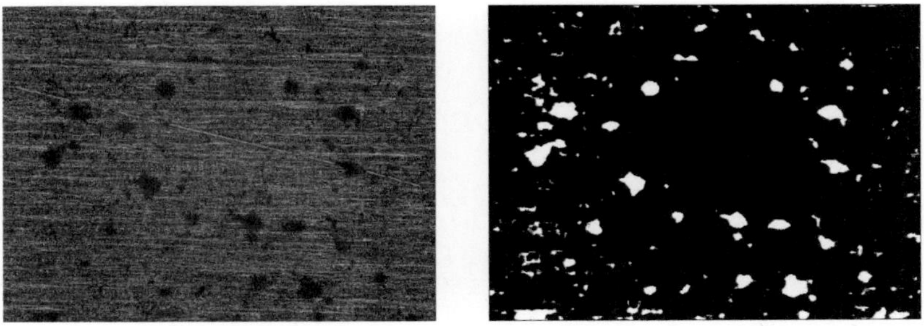

Figure 3.1: Textured metal surface with contaminations (left) and detected contamination (right).

		Accuracy
Thresholding		70.2%
Bi-orthogonal spline wavelet 3.5		68.4%
$MCFB$	C_s	84.5%
$RWFB$	$C_s, t = 1$	94.5%
$RWFB$	$C_s, t = 2$	95.2%
$RWFB$	$C_s, t = 3$	96.4%

Table 3.2: Accuracy using different wavelet filter banks for classification of the class *stain* C_s.

4 Conclusion

In this paper two different designing methods for wavelet filter banks were introduced. By the first method *MCFB* the filter bank was optimized on the profile of defect. The second method *RWFB* optimized the filter bank not only on the profile of defect but also on the most dominant stretchings of defect. Both optimization methods were evaluated with two task within the image processing: measured data from deflectometry and stain on metal surfaces. With better classification and detection rates the new methods proved their advantage over other traditional methods. Among the two methods the *RWFB* was superior to proposed *MCFB* method.

This work was part of a project financed by the Baden-Württemberg Stiftung.

Bibliography

[Blu98] T. Blu. A new design algorithm for two-band orthonormal rational filter banks and orthonormal rational wavelets. *IEEE Trans. Signal Processing*, 46(6):1494–1504, 1998.

[BS09a] I. Bayram and I.W. Selesnick. Frequency-domain design of overcomplete rational-dilation wavelet transforms. *IEEE Trans. Signal Processing*, 57(8):2957–2972, 2009.

[CDF06] A. Cohen, I. Daubechies, and J.C. Feauveau. Biorthogonal bases of compactly supported wavelets. *Communications on Pure and Applied Mathematics*, 45(5):485–560, 2006.

[Gre96] T. Greiner. Orthogonal and biorthogonal texture-matched wavelet filterbanks for hierarchical texture analysis. *Signal Processing*, 54(1):1–22, 1996.

[Le14] Tan-Toan Le. Wavelet filter bank optimization for classification of deflectometry measuring data. In *Proceedings of the 2013 Joint Workshop of Fraunhofer IOSB and Institute for Anthropomatics, Vision and Fusion Laboratory*, volume 17, page 41. KIT Scientific Publishing, 2014.

[Li09] T.-S. Li. Applying wavelets transform, rough set theory and support vector machine for copper clad laminate defects classification. *Expert Systems with Applications*, 36:5822–5829, 2009.

[NN13] S.T.N. Nguyen and B.W.-H. Ng. Bi-orthogonal rational discrete wavelet transform with multiple regularity orders and application experiments. *Signal Processing*, 93(11):3014 – 3026, 2013.

[Vet86] M. Vetterli. Filter banks allowing perfect reconstruction. *Signal Processing*, 10(3):219–244, 1986.

[WN99] Y. Wisutmethangoon and T. Q. Nguyen. A method for design of mth-band filters. *IEEE Trans. Signal Processing*, 47(6):1669–1678, 1999.

[ZLGH12] M. Ziebarth, T.-T. Le, T. Greiner, and M. Heizmann. Inspektion spiegelnder Oberflächen mit Wavelet-basierten Verfahren. In Michael Puente León, Fernando; Heizmann, editor, *Forum Bildverarbeitung 2012*, pages 167–180, Regensburg, Deutschland, November 2012. KIT Scientific Publishing.

Visual Inspection of Transparent Objects Physical Basics, Existing Methods and Novel Ideas

Johannes Meyer

Vision and Fusion Laboratory
Institute for Anthropomatics
Karlsruhe Institute of Technology (KIT), Germany
johannes.meyer@kit.edu

Technical Report IES-2014-04

Abstract: Various industries, e. g., manufacturers of optical components or medical equipment, use components made out of transparent materials to craft devices for high-precision applications. As this involves the need for fulfilling high quality assurances, any kind of defect like enclosed air bubbles, contaminants or cracks, has to be reliably detected. Much effort has been spent and is currently spent into developing methods suitable for visually inspecting transparent objects. In contrast to opaque objects, transparent materials pose various challenging problems, as any light ray involved in the inspection process can be reflected and refracted by the investigated sample, complicating the design of the setup and of the method used for the inspection. On the one hand, this report gives an introduction to the specific physical properties of interest of transparent objects. On the other hand, it provides an overview over existing methods used for capturing these properties and describes sketches of some novel inspection approaches.

1 Introduction

The inspection of transparent objects is very important for various industries. For example, windshields and headlight glasses of automobiles have to be checked for cracks or impurities which might impair the sight of the driver or cause instabilities. In food industry, glass bottles or other food containers have to be checked for being impermeable and free from contaminants. Besides, plastic lenses used for laser-supported eye surgery have to be inspected to ensure certain quality requirements. Furthermore, optical elements themselves, as they are used in optical instruments, have to be inspected, in order to check whether they meet their specifications.

In contrast to transparent objects, there exist various methods suitable for inspecting opaque or specular objects. This report introduces the characteristic optical properties of transparent objects, discusses possible defects related to these properties and covers the corresponding challenges of inspection. Besides, rough sketches of some novel inspection approaches are presented.

2 Properties of Transparent Objects

As for any object, the properties of transparent objects can be divided into the two groups of optical properties and 3D geometry, which are presented in the following two sections.

2.1 3D Geometry

The 3D geometry of a transparent object refers to its outer shape. Depending on the object on hand and on the visual inspection task, the complete reconstruction of the object is required or differences between the test object and a reference object, e. g., defects, have to detected. For example, glass or plastic lenses used for optical imaging only produce the desired images if their 3D geometry exactly matches the specifications, which is why a complete reconstruction of their outer shape would be necessary for their inspection.

Common methods used for visually obtaining the geometry of opaque objects are based on triangulation, optical path lengths or intensity measurements. However, most of these methods cannot be directly applied to transparent objects, as most of the incident light is transmitted and nearly no light is reflected.

Triangulation approaches usually rely on the calculation of a missing side of the triangle consisting of a (laser) light source, the illuminated spot on the test object and the sensor observing the test object [Nol07]. The missing side is mostly the distance of the sensor and the current measurement spot on the test object. As the surface of a transparent object shows barely no reflections and transmits most of the incident light, there is no clearly visible illuminated spot that can be seen by the sensor. As this is also the case for any pattern projection or Moire method, triangulation is not suitable for obtaining the 3D geometry of transparent objects.

Methods based on measuring the length of the optical path of light (LIDAR [Cam02], interferometry [Har92], shearography [SY03], holography [Kre05]), which is sent to the object and which is observed after being reflected, also require the test object to reflect a certain amount of the incident light, which is why they are not suitable for transparent objects either.

In contrast, methods based on capturing the intensity of light transmitted by transparent objects might be suitable for obtaining the object's 3D geometry. One of these methods – the shape from silhouette approach – is described in section 3.1. However, it has yet not been used to acquire the 3D shape of transparent objects. Therefore, a simple but novel approach using shape from silhouette is presented in 4.1.

2.2 Optical Properties

Furthermore, also optical properties might be of interest. These include the refraction index and the color of the test object. Depending on the requirements of the actual application, the color of the transparent object, i. e., light of which wavelengths is absorbed or transmitted by the object can be determined by observing the light transmitted by the test object with a color camera or with a spectrally resolving sensor [Cha03]. As the visual appearance and the optical effects of transparent objects are mainly caused by light being deflected during transmission, the spatial distribution of the refraction index is of special importance.

Refraction occurs if light passes the boundary between two adjacent media with different refraction indices n_1 and n_2. If the angle of incidence of the incident light ray in medium 1 is denoted by θ_1 with respect to the normal of the boundary layer and if θ_2 is the corresponding angle of the emitted light ray in medium 2, Snell's law of refraction holds:

$$n_1 \sin\theta_1 = n_2 \sin\theta_2 \,.$$

The effect of refraction is illustrated in Fig. 2.1. If it is $\theta_1 = 0°$, it holds $\theta_2 = 0°$. For exact calculations, the refraction index has to be considered as a function of the light's wavelength λ:

$$n = n(\lambda)\,.$$

This dependency is called dispersion. If the material of the transparent object is inhomogeneous, the refraction index might even be a function of the position $\mathbf{x} \in \mathbb{R}^3$:

$$n = n(\lambda, \mathbf{x})\,.$$

The refraction index can be measured, e. g., by means of the Schlieren imaging method described in Sect. 3.2.

Material defects affecting the refraction index can result in serious consequences: for example, small enclosed air bubbles or contaminants inside a transparent plastic lens used for a laser-supported eye surgery might cause the laser to be directed into the wrong direction and therefore to harm the patient. Such defects can be

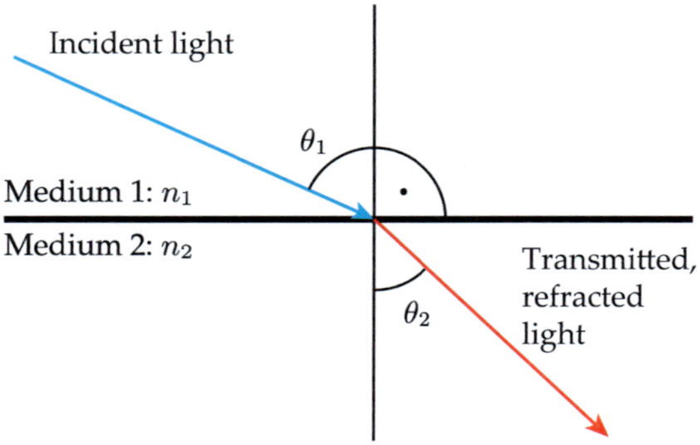

Figure 2.1: Snell's law of refraction.

detected as local inhomogeneities of the refraction index or as sources of scattered light if illuminated in dark field.

3 Existing Methods

In this section, two existing methods for inspecting transparent objects are presented. Besides their basic principle, also the drawbacks of the methods will be mentioned.

3.1 Shape from Silhouette

Shape from silhouette is a method which is able to approximate the 3D shape of opaque objects by combining views of its silhouette captured out of different projection directions [TCM+02]. To simplify matters, only two dimensions will be considered for explaining the approach. Figure 3.1 illustrates the setup for capturing an object's silhouette out of a single projection direction. As the light source is placed in the focal point of the lens L_1, the object is illuminated with parallel light, so that the object's silhouette is visible on the sensor. The setup is now rotated around the object in order to capture silhouettes out of multiple perspectives. As the rotation angles are known and the illumination is calibrated with respect to the sensor, the path of the two rays which are just 'touching' the borders of the object can be reconstructed and the rectangular area between these two rays can be intersected with the other rectangles corresponding to the different projection directions. By this means, a step-wise approximation of the outer shape of the

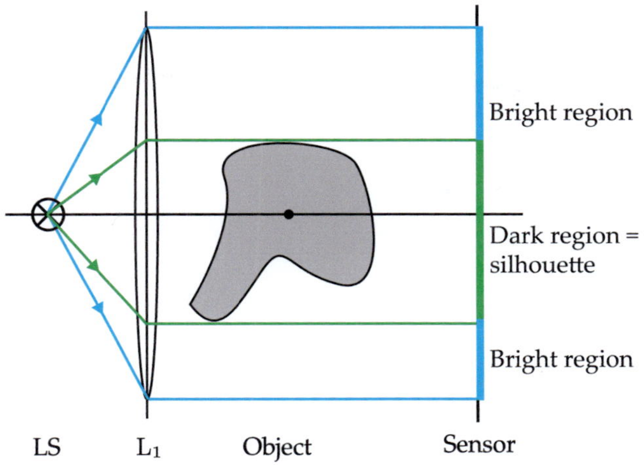

Figure 3.1: Visualization of the optical setup used for shape from silhouette. A light source LS is placed in the focal point of the lens L_1, so that only parallel light reaches the investigated object. As the object is opaque, its silhouette corresponding to the current projection direction is imaged to the sensor and appears as a dark region.

investigated object can be obtained (see Figure 3.2). The more projections directions are used the more exact the resulting approximation will be. As rectangles are convex geometric objects, an intersection of two rectangles will always result in another convex object [Cop98]. This is why – theoretically – shape from silhouette can only achieve a perfect reconstruction of convex objects and any concave structures on the surface of the investigated objects will never be contained in the reconstruction (see Figure 3.2).

In the three-dimensional case, the single two-dimensional projections are polygons, which do not necessarily have to be convex. The results of the corresponding intersections can be arbitrary polyhedra that do not have any inner structures like cavities. Unfortunately, the intersection of three-dimensional polyhedra is very complex and computationally expensive. Besides, as it is presented here, shape from silhouette gives much better results for opaque objects than for transparent objects, as only the contours of transparent objects would be visible as slightly darker structures on the sensor. In Sect. 4.1, an approach is proposed which possibly resolves this drawback.

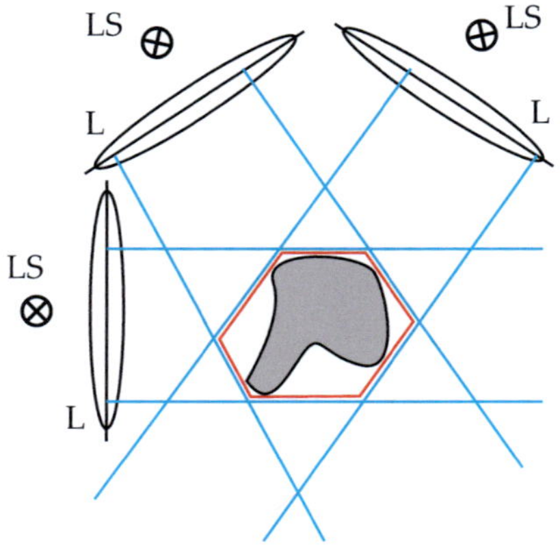

Figure 3.2: The setup shown in Fig. 3.1 is used for multiple projection directions. For every configuration, the two rays touching the object are colored blue. The red polygon, which is the intersection of the rectangular areas between the pairs of rays, presents a convex approximation of the shape of the investigated object.

3.2 Schlieren Imaging

As mentioned above, light rays do not follow a straight line when passing a transparent object with varying refraction index. As this effect can be measured, information about the refraction index can be gained [Sch95]. In order to obtain an intensity image representing the deflection of the rays, a so-called schlieren stop can be used, which is placed asymmetrically into the optical path. By this means, the deflection of the light rays results in a varying intensity on the image sensor. Figure 3.3 shows the principal setup used for schlieren imaging. The setup is sensitive for changes of the refraction index perpendicular to the edge of the schlieren stop. In order to obtain information about different directions of the gradient of the refraction index, images with different configurations of the schlieren stop have to be captured or a color wheel can be placed in the focal point of L_2, which allows a color encoding of the deflection direction.

Another variant of schlieren imaging uses a certain '4D' background illumination, which utilizes micro lenses in order to achieve a color encoding of the spatial position of each illuminating element and of the outgoing direction. By this means, the test object can be placed just in front of this background and common consumer cameras can be used to obtain a qualitative schlieren image [WRH11].

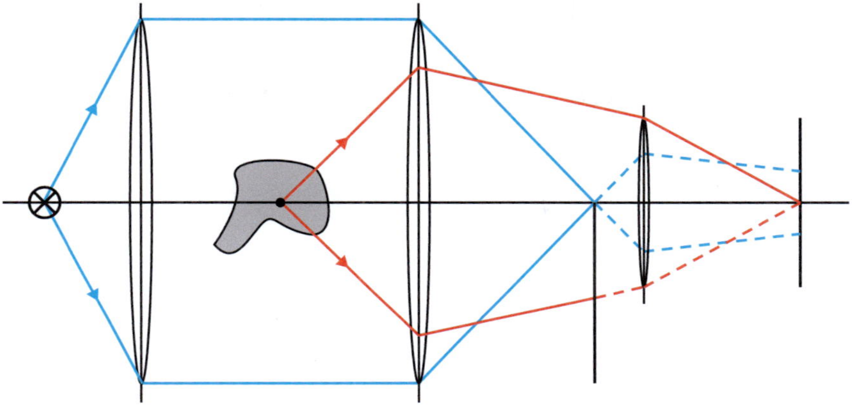

Figure 3.3: Principle of schlieren imaging. The light of the light source LS is collimated by L_1 and illuminates the investigated transparent object. The collimated light is focused by the lens L_2. A schlieren stop SS is located in the focal point of L_2, ideally halving the luminance if no test object is present. Light rays deflected upwards (downwards) by the test object are able to pass the schlieren stop (are blocked) and result in high (low) values output by the sensor. The resulting intensity images are called 'schlieren'. By means of the lenses L_2 and L_3, a focused imaging of the object onto the sensor is realized.

As already mentioned, a single configuration of the original schlieren setup only allows to obtain information about the components of the refraction index distribution, which are perpendicular to the edge of the schlieren stop. Section 4.2 outlines a novel approach which could possibly resolve this drawback.

4 Novel Approaches

In this section, two novel ideas are presented, which extend the methods shape from silhouette and schlieren imaging to better suit transparent objects.

4.1 Shape from Silhouette for Transparent Objects

As discussed in Sect. 3.1, the shape from silhouette method is not directly suitable for obtaining the outer shape of transparent objects. The problem is, that the inspected object should be opaque, so that its silhouette is represented by a thorough, dark region on the image sensor. The contrast with which the contour of a transparent object would be visible, might be low, resulting in inaccurate silhouette measurements.

Figure 4.1 shows the sketch of a setup which could possibly be used to capture the single silhouette projections of transparent objects. The original setup from Fig. 3.1 is extended by another lens and a telecentric stop which is placed in this lens' focal point. By this means, only rays running parallel to the optical axis between the two lenses are able to pass the telecentric stop and to reach the image sensor. Any ray running through the transparent object will be refracted when entering or leaving the object or when traversing inner structures of the object, so that it will not be parallel to optical axis anymore and will be blocked by the telecentric stop. The image formed on the sensor should show the silhouette of the object corresponding to the configured projection direction. By utilizing this setup, the shape from silhouette method (Sect. 3.1) should be applicable to transparent objects as well as to opaque objects. However, there still are some transparent objects which could be problematic for this method, e. g., a transparent cuboid which is arranged so that its sides are exactly parallel or perpendicular to the optical axis resulting in no refraction of some of the rays and therefore in an unusable sensor image. But as this case is very unlikely and as objects are rotated during the inspection, the approach could still be successful for such object classes.

4.2 Variable Stop Schlieren Imaging

As mentioned in Sect. 3.2, the schlieren method can be used to visualize the refraction index of transparent objects as intensity images. However, the method is only sensitive for refraction index gradients perpendicular to the edge of the schlieren stop as it is aligned in the current setup.

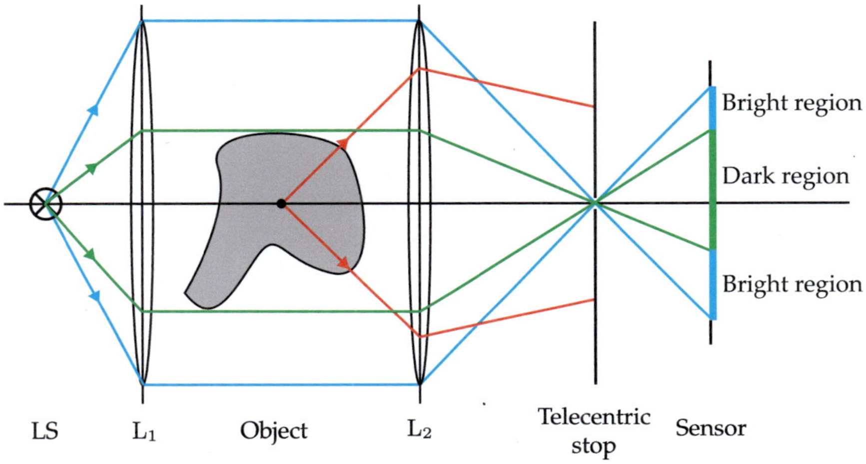

Figure 4.1: A setup allowing to apply shape from silhouette to transparent objects. The setup from Fig. 3.1 is extended by an additional lens L_2 and a telecentric stop which is placed in the focal point of L_2. By this means, only rays parallel to the optical axis are able to reach the sensor and any ray coming in contact with the transparent object and getting refracted will be blocked by the telecentric stop.

By using a highly variable and controllable schlieren stop and by acquiring an image series whose images correspond to the configurations of the schlieren stop, the refraction index field could possibly be sampled. Figure 4.2 illustrates a possible setup. Here, a so-called digital micromirror device (DMD) is used to realize the variable schlieren stop. A DMD is a rectangular array of for example $2 \cdot 10^6$ mirrors having a size of about $10\mu\text{m} \cdot 10\mu\text{m}$ [Ins15]. Every single mirror can be electrically tilted by several discrete angles with a frequency of 400 MHz. By this means, the single elements can be turned 'on' or 'off', i. e., they can be set to direct the light in the correct direction towards L_3 or out of the optical system. Thus, the DMD can be used to realize various stop configurations and a series of images containing information about the refraction index gradients in the corresponding direction can be acquired.

5 Conclusion

This report introduced the physical basics regarding the visual inspection of transparent objects and the associated challenges. The suitability of existing visual inspection methods for the inspection of transparent objects has been discussed and

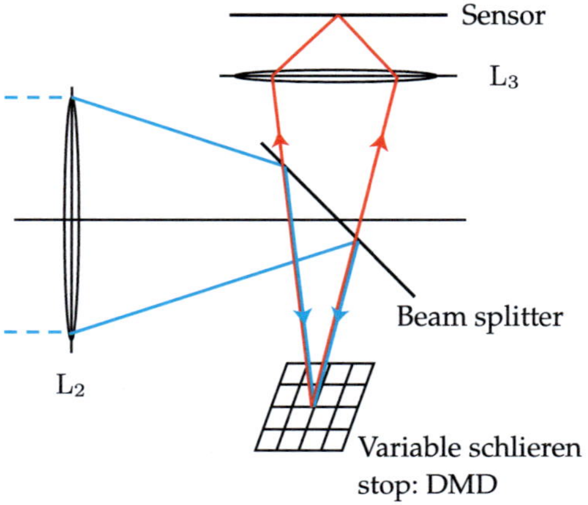

Figure 4.2: Principle of schlieren imaging realizing a variable schlieren stop. The figure has to be considered as an extension of the part right from the lens L_2 in Figure 3.3. To simplify matters, the deflected rays are neglected. Here, a beam splitter is placed in the optical path beyond the lens L_2. After being reflected by the beam splitter, the light reaches a digital micromirror device (DMD), which replaces the schlieren stop of the original setup. This DMD is controlled by a computer to realize different schlieren stop configurations $S_1, S_2, \ldots, S_N$ at different points of time $t_1, t_2, \ldots, t_N$. The sensor is triggered to acquire images $I_1, I_2, \ldots, I_N$ at the respective points of time t_i.

two novel ideas have been presented: on the one hand, an image acquisition setup has been proposed, which possibly allows the application of shape from silhouette to transparent objects and on the other hand, an expansion of the schlieren method has been presented, which utilizes a variable schlieren stop in order to gain more information about the investigated object.

Now, these approaches need to be physically realized and evaluated by means of theoretically well-grounded experiments.

Bibliography

[Cam02] James B. Campbell. *Introduction to remote sensing*. Guilford Press New York, 3rd edition, 2002.

[Cha03] Chein-I Chang. *Hyperspectral imaging : techniques for spectral detection and classification*. Kluwer Academic, 2003.

[Cop98] William A. Coppel. *Foundations of convex geometry*. Australian Mathematical Society lecture series ; 12. Cambridge University Press, 1st edition, 1998.

[Har92] Parameswaran Hariharan. *Basics of interferometry*. Academic Press, 1992.

[Ins15] Texas Instruments. *DLPS025B, http://www.ti.com/lit/ds/symlink/dlp9500.pdf*, 2012 (accessed January 7, 2015).

[Kre05] Thomas Kreis. *Handbook of holographic interferometry : optical and digital methods*. WILEY-VCH, 2005.

[Nol07] Reinhard Noll. Lasertriangulation. In Norbert Bauer, editor, *Handbuch zur Industriellen Bildverarbeitung*, pages 56–60. Fraunhofer IRB Verlag, Stuttgart, 1st edition, 2007.

[Sch95] Alexander Schwarz. *Multitomographische Temperaturmessung in Flammen mit einem Schlierenmeßaufbau*. PhD thesis, Universität Karlsruhe (TH), 1995.

[SY03] Wolfgang Steinchen and Lianxiang Yang. *Digital shearography : theory and application of digital Speckle pattern shearing interferometry*. SPIE Optical Engineering Press, 2003.

[TCM+02] Marco Tarini, Marco Callieri, Claudio Montani, Claudio Rocchini, Karin Olsson, and Therese Persson. Marching intersections: An efficient approach to shape-from-silhouette. In *VMV*, pages 283–290, 2002.

[WRH11] Gordon Wetzstein, Ramesh Raskar, and Wolfgang Heidrich. Hand-held schlieren photography with light field probes. In *Computational Photography (ICCP), 2011 IEEE International Conference on*, pages 1–8. IEEE, 2011.

Thickness Measurement of Thin Films on Curved Surfaces with Ellipsometry

Christian Negara

Fraunhofer Institute of Optronics,
System Technologies and Image Exploitation IOSB
Fraunhoferstr. 1, 76131 Karlsruhe, Germany
christian.negara@iosb.fraunhofer.de

Technical Report IES-2014-05

Abstract: Ellipsometry is a proven method for measuring layer thicknesses of flat, specularly reflective surfaces from the angstrom up to the micrometer range. At the Fraunhofer IOSB a new measuring system has been developed which allows the application of imaging ellipsometry on curved surfaces. The light beam is reflected twice off the sample surface, hence the ellipsometry measurements change but they are directly related to the measurements of conventional single wavelength ellipsomety. Several problems arise when interpreting the ellipsometry measurements from the new measurement system, like unknown angle of incidence, few measurements per pixel and often unknown materials. In this article these problems are identified and some steps are proposed to be able to apply imaging ellipsometry on curved surfaces for special applications. Currently, the focus remains on isotropic samples consisting of a single layer on a substrate.

1 Introduction

In many production processes for e.g. semiconductors, optical components, photonics, automobile parts but also household appliances, thin film coatings are used to obtain the desired functionality of the product. Ellipsometry is a non-destructive, contact-free, optical measurement technique which is widely used for material characterization and thickness measurement of thin films. Material characterization is performed with spectroscopic ellipsometry, where measurements at different wavelengths are acquired. One restriction of ellipsometry is, that the surface under study has to be partially reflective and the layers must not be opaque. The principal configuration of an ellipsometer is explained in Section 4. The light source and the detector must be adjusted in such a way according to the surface normal, that the reflection condition holds. This implies that only flat surfaces can be examined because at every change in inclination the sensor and detector have to be repositioned. For point sensors there exist extensions for small inclinations of the surface normal [NR02, FGS+95]. Additionally, the field of view of actual imaging ellipsometers is very small (less than $2.5\ \mathrm{cm}$ in diameter). Hence, imaging ellipsometry is usually used in conjunction with microscopy.

The new and patented ellipsometry measurement system developed at the Fraunhofer IOSB [Fra] overcomes these drawbacks by taking advantage of the retroreflection. The light source and the detector are combined into a transceiver and the reflection condition is automatically fulfilled as shown in Section 5. The usage of a laser scanner avoids the depth of field problem inherent to imaging ellipsometry and the field of view of actual imaging ellipsometers is also drastically extended by the use of a $20\ \mathrm{cm}$ wide laser line. This opens up the possibility to measure thin films on curved surfaces with ellipsometry such as coatings on automobile parts, metal rolls or painted plastic parts. In these applications the variation of the layer thickness over the sample surface is of interest while the number of layers is usually low. There is often little knowledge about the materials used in these applications, in contrast to classical applications of ellipsometry, e.g. semiconductor industry, where the detected materials are known very well. Additionally, although measurements can be acquired on curved surfaces, the angle of incidence is unknown - in contrast to the classical ellipsometry approach. This requires that either a CAD model of the inspected part is available or the topography is measured with supplemental 3D sensors.

As a model-based approach, ellipsometry cannot be used to measure the layer thicknesses directly without some sort of knowledge about the number of layers or the optical properties of the materials. The model to be determined consists of a layer stack with specific materials and layer thicknesses. Before analyzing a sample with the new ellipsometry scanner, the first step is to measure the optical properties and the number of layers with spectroscopic ellipsometry at a fixed location on the sample. This is done so, because spectroscopic ellipsometry provides more measurements as is the case with the monochromatic (red) laser scanner. Hence, it is more likely to derive the correct model. This is especially in our use cases important, where there is usually little knowledge about the materials of the sample. To further increase the confidence in the model parameters, variable angle spectroscopic ellipsomety (VASE) is applied by acquiring spectroscopic measurements at different angles of incidence. Section 6 of this article addresses the problem of obtaining a model from VASE measurements of an isotropic sample consisting of a single layer on a substrate. Instead of using real VASE measurements, they are simulated using an existing ellipsometry software (DeltaPsi2) to generate ground truth data from a known model.

The fitting of the model parameters is achieved via a nonlinear optimization. Given a known model, the ellipsometric parameters are computed and compared with the measured values (i.e. simulated values). The model is then successively updated and improved until the stopping condition is satisfied. One part of the optimization algorithm is the computation of the ellipsometric parameters from a given model. Section 2 addresses some theoretical aspects of polarized light and polarization change due to reflection. In Section 3 an algorithm for computing the ellipsometric parameters for the reflection at an arbitrary layer stack is explained.

After determining the number of layers, the materials and the layer thicknesses with VASE at a specific point on the surface, the variation of the layer thickness over the sample surface can be measured with the ellipsometry scanner. To be able to apply methods from classical ellipsometry to fit the model parameters to measurements obtained with the ellipsometry scanner, the measurements from both ellipsometry systems have to be compared. A relationship between these measurements is presented in Section 5 and occurring model-fitting ambiguities are discussed.

2 Polarization of light

Light is an electromagnetic wave, which can be regarded as a homogenous plane wave for describing the polarization state of light. The direction and magnitude of the electric and magnetic field vector alternate as the light propagates through space. In the further analysis only the electric field vector is used. Let $\boldsymbol{E}(z,t)$ denote the electric field vector at position z and time t. Polarized light is in the general case elliptically polarized. In this case the electric field vector moves along the curve of an ellipse in the xy-plane as it propagates through space in z direction as shown in Figure 2.1. The polarization state of light can be decomposed into two orthogonal states. The figure shows the decomposition of an elliptically polarized light wave into two linear polarized light waves while the vibration planes are the xz- and the yz-plane. The electric field vectors $E_x(z,t)$ and $E_y(z,t)$ can be either expressed as real-valued functions $E(z,t) = A \cdot cos(k_z z - \omega t + \varphi)$ or as complex ones $\underline{E}(t) = A \cdot \exp(i(k_z z - \omega t + \varphi))$, whereas k_z is the circular wavenumber, ω the angular frequency, A the amplitude and φ the initial phase. The complex notation will be used in the following sections.

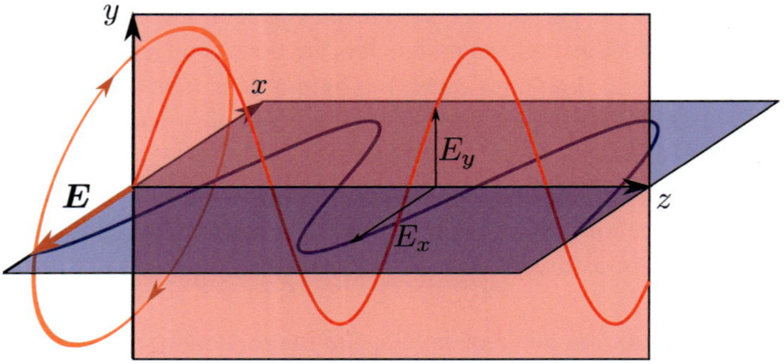

Figure 2.1: Decomposition of an elliptically polarized light wave by two linearly polarized waves.

3 Reflection

The reflection and refraction of light at a flat boundary surface of two isotropic theoretically semi-infinite materials is determined by the Fresnel equations [TM99]. These formulas describe the change of the amplitude and phase of the electric field vector of the incident and reflected light ray resulting from the reflection or refraction. As mentioned in the previous section, light with an arbitrary polarization state can be decomposed into two orthogonal linearly polarized light rays. If the vibration planes are parallel (p-polarization) and perpendicular (s-polarization) to the plane of incidence, the change in amplitude and phase can be computed separately for the two polarization states. The plane of incidence is being spanned by the direction vector of the incident light ray and the surface normal. Let the complex values $\underline{E}_i^s, \underline{E}_i^p$ denote the amplitude and phase of the incident light ray for the s- and p-polarization and let $\underline{E}_r^s, \underline{E}_r^p$ denote the amplitude and phase of the reflected ray. The reflection coefficients are defined by:

$$\underline{r}_{12}^p = \frac{\underline{E}_r^p}{\underline{E}_i^p}, \underline{r}_{12}^s = \frac{\underline{E}_r^s}{\underline{E}_i^s}.$$

The vectors of the electric fields of the incident and reflected ray are depicted in Figure 3.1 for the p- and s-polarization. Let θ_1 be the angle of incidence in medium 1 and θ_2 the angle of refraction in medium 2. The refractive index n and the extinction coefficient k of a material can be expressed as the complex refractive index $\underline{n} = n - ik$. Let $\underline{n}_1, \underline{n}_2$ denote the complex refractive index of the medium 1 and medium 2, respectively. The reflection coefficients can be computed with the

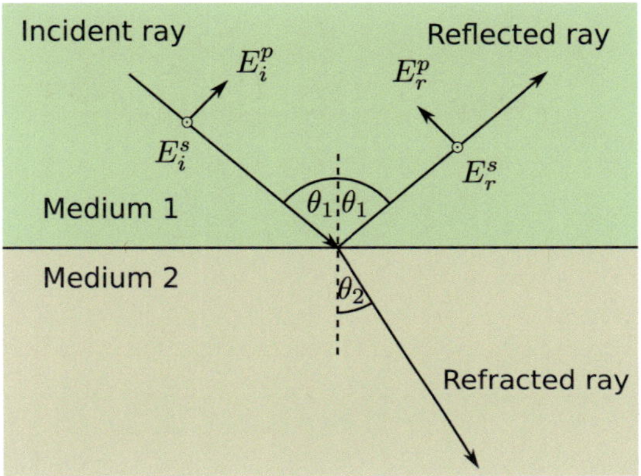

Figure 3.1: Reflection and refraction of light at a flat boundary surface.

help of the Fresnel equations:

$$\begin{aligned}\underline{r}_{12}^p &= \frac{\underline{n}_2 \cos\underline{\theta}_1 - \underline{n}_1 \cos\underline{\theta}_2}{\underline{n}_2 \cos\underline{\theta}_1 + \underline{n}_1 \cos\underline{\theta}_2},\\ \underline{r}_{12}^s &= \frac{\underline{n}_1 \cos\underline{\theta}_1 - \underline{n}_2 \cos\underline{\theta}_2}{\underline{n}_1 \cos\underline{\theta}_1 + \underline{n}_2 \cos\underline{\theta}_2}.\end{aligned} \tag{3.1}$$

$\underline{\theta}_2$ can be computed using Snell's law:

$$\underline{n}_1 \sin\underline{\theta}_1 = \underline{n}_2 \sin\underline{\theta}_2. \tag{3.2}$$

Because transmission ellipsometry used at transparent objects is not a subject of this article, the Fresnel equations for the refracted rays are omitted.

When there is a layer between the two semi-infinite media with flat parallel boundary surfaces, the light beam is reflected or refracted at the two interfaces as shown in Figure 3.2. The phase of a partial beam which is refracted from medium 2 into medium 1 after one or multiple reflections depends on the thickness d, the number of reflections that occurred and the complex refractive indices $\underline{n}_1, \underline{n}_2, \underline{n}_3$. All these partial beams superimpose and by summing an infinite geometric series we obtain the following formula for the two reflection coefficients:

$$\begin{aligned}\underline{r}_{123}^p &= \frac{\underline{r}_{12}^p + \underline{r}_{23}^p e^{-i2\underline{\beta}}}{1 + \underline{r}_{12}^p \underline{r}_{23}^p e^{-i2\underline{\beta}}},\\ \underline{r}_{123}^s &= \frac{\underline{r}_{12}^s + \underline{r}_{23}^s e^{-i2\underline{\beta}}}{1 + \underline{r}_{12}^s \underline{r}_{23}^s e^{-i2\underline{\beta}}},\end{aligned} \tag{3.3}$$

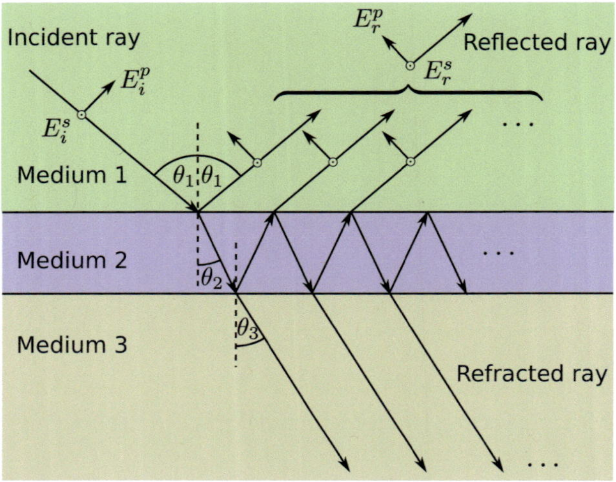

Figure 3.2: Because of the presence of a layer, the polarization state of the output beam is composed of partial beams reflected at both interfaces.

where

$$\underline{\beta} = 2\pi \left(\frac{d}{\lambda}\right) \underline{n}_2 \cos \underline{\theta}_2.$$

One simple method of computing the total reflection coefficient for an arbitrary number of layers is to use Equation (3.3) recursively [TM99]. As seen in Figure 3.2 the effect of the layer on the polarization state of an incident beam can be treated as if there was only a substrate with no layer by using the total reflection coefficients. With Equation (3.3) it is possible to successively add a layer on top to get the total reflection coefficients of the whole stack:

$$\begin{aligned} \underline{r}^p_{j\ldots n} &= \frac{\underline{r}^p_{j,j+1} + \underline{r}^p_{j+1\ldots n} \mathrm{e}^{-i2\underline{\beta}}}{1 + \underline{r}^p_{j,j+1} \underline{r}^p_{j+1\ldots n} \mathrm{e}^{-i2\underline{\beta}}}, \\ \underline{r}^s_{j\ldots n} &= \frac{\underline{r}^s_{j,j+1} + \underline{r}^s_{j+1\ldots n} \mathrm{e}^{-i2\underline{\beta}}}{1 + \underline{r}^s_{j,j+1} \underline{r}^s_{j+1\ldots n} \mathrm{e}^{-i2\underline{\beta}}}, \end{aligned} \tag{3.4}$$

where

$$\underline{\beta} = 2\pi \left(\frac{d_{j+1}}{\lambda}\right) \underline{n}_{j+1} \cos \underline{\theta}_{j+1}$$

and d_j is the thickness of layer j and $\underline{\theta}_j$ the angle of incidence of a beam inside layer j. $\underline{r}^p_{j,j+1}, \underline{r}^s_{j,j+1}$ is defined as in Equation (3.1). It is worth to note that Equation (3.1), (3.2), (3.3), (3.4) are not only valid for real refractive indices but also for complex ones (except of $\underline{n}_1$) [TM99]. The sin and cos functions can be extended to the complex domain through Euler's formula:

$$\sin \underline{x} = \frac{\exp^{i\underline{x}} - \exp^{-i\underline{x}}}{2i}, \cos \underline{x} = \frac{\exp^{i\underline{x}} + \exp^{-i\underline{x}}}{2}.$$

For the computation of the complex angle of refraction using Equation (3.2), the arcsin function for the complex domain is needed. The arcsin function can be extended to the complex domain through the complex logarithm:

$$\arcsin(x) = -i \ln\left(i\, x + \sqrt{1 - x^2}\right).$$

4 Spectroscopic Ellipsometry

In spectroscopic reflectometry the thickness of a layer is computed by measuring the interference spectrum of a light beam reflected off a sample surface - usually at normal incidence. When the sample consists of one or multiple layers, the partial beams are reflected at each interface. These reflected partial beams superimpose which results in an interference spectrum dependent on the optical properties and the thicknesses of the layers. At normal incidence the s- and p-polarization cannot be determined and at a non-depolarizing, isotropic sample, the polarization state of the incident light is preserved. In contrast to reflectometry, in ellipsometry the change of the polarization state resulting from the reflection is measured while the angle of incidence θ is usually near the Brewster angle.

An ellipsometer consists of a light source, a detector and optical elements like linear polarizers and retarders or quarter-wave plates also called compensators which can be rotated [TM99]. These are used to generate a polarization state at the input beam or to measure the polarization state of the output beam. The principal configuration of an ellipsometer is depicted in Figure 4.1. The angle ϕ denotes the rotation of the sensor coordinate system with respect to the plane of incidence. With a fixed analyzer and a rotating compensator at the output beam, the polarization state of the reflected light can be detected by measuring at four azimuthal angles [BPLF12] of the compensator. With spectroscopic ellipsometry, measurements are acquired for every wavelength. The spectrum used for the simulations in 6.1 corresponds to the spectrum of the SmartSE ellipsometer from Horiba and ranges from $400 - 1000$ nm.

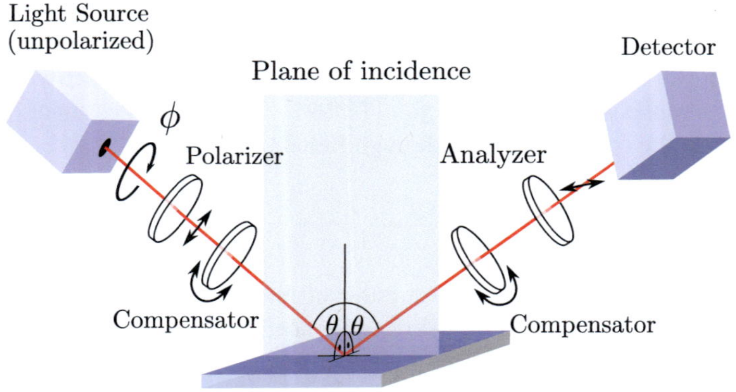

Figure 4.1: Ellipsometer configuration with rotating compensators.

4.1 Ellipsometry parameters Psi and Delta

Two important ellipsometry parameters usually used for model fitting are Ψ and Δ which can be expressed as the complex value $\underline{\rho}$. Ψ describe the change in the amplitude quotient and Δ the change in the phase difference of two orthogonal linearly polarized waves. Because the coordinate system of the ellipsometer is adjusted according to the plane of incidence ($\phi = 0$), the two linearly polarized waves correspond to the s- and p-polarization. The ellipsometric parameters Ψ, Δ are then related to the reflection coefficients by the fundamental equation of ellipsometry [TM99]:

$$\underline{\rho} := \tan \Psi \mathrm{e}^{i\Delta} = \frac{\underline{r}^p}{\underline{r}^s}. \tag{4.1}$$

With Ψ and Δ, the optical properties of a substrate can directly be determined. A substrate is a thick bulk material where no back-side reflection occurs. Let $\underline{n}_1$ be the complex refractive index of the ambient and $\underline{n}_2$ the complex refractive index of the substrate. In Figure 4.2 for fixed refractive indices n and variable extinction coefficients k the corresponding Ψ, Δ trajectories are shown. For $k = 0$ the trajectory begins at $\Delta \in \{0°, 180°\}$ when there is no total internal reflection and ends at $\Psi = 45°, \Delta = 180°$ for $k \to \infty$. As can be seen, there is a one-to-one correspondence between n, k and Ψ, Δ if θ_1 is fixed. The complex refractive index $\underline{n}_2$ can be computed from Ψ, Δ by [TM99]:

$$\underline{n}_2 = \underline{n}_1 \tan \theta_1 \sqrt{1 - \frac{4\underline{\rho} \sin^2 \theta_1}{(\underline{\rho} + 1)^2}}. \tag{4.2}$$

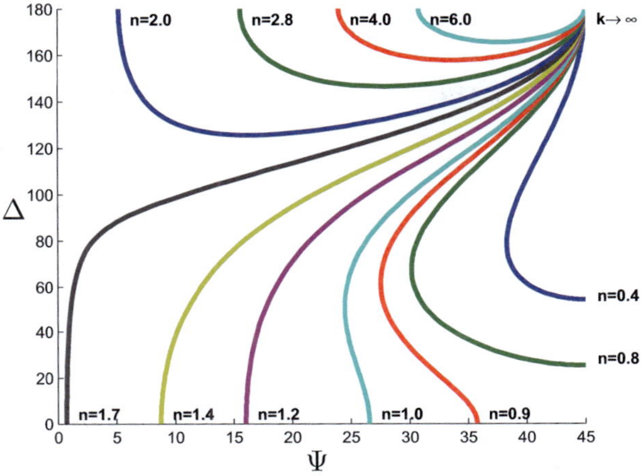

Figure 4.2: Ψ and Δ for different n, k at $\theta = 60°$ and $\lambda = 635$ nm.

When there is a layer on the surface, the situation is more complicated. As can be seen in Equation (3.3) the total reflection coefficients are periodic in thickness d for a transparent film. In this case the refractive index is real $\underline{n}_2 = n_2$. Additionally, $n_2 > 1$ for nearly all natural materials in the visible wavelength range. For a given (real-valued) angle of incidence $\underline{\theta}_1 = \theta_1$, $\underline{\theta}_2$ and $\underline{\beta}$ are also real according to Equation (3.2) if air is assumed as the ambient $n_1 = 1$. This results into a periodic function of the total reflection coefficient in the thickness d. The period has the same order of magnitude as the wavelength which is below 1 μm when using a red laser. To be able to detect thicknesses in the μm-range, either λ has to be varied, as is the case with spectroscopic ellipsometry, or θ_1, as is the case with the ellipsometry scanner. This leads to an unambiguity of the thickness d because the period d_p is a function of λ and θ_1 [TM99]:

$$d_p = \frac{\lambda}{2\sqrt{n_2^2 - n_1^2 \sin^2 \theta_1}}.$$

Many fitting procedures in ellipsometry assume that the sample under study consists of multiple parallel layers. Even in cases when the surface is rough or the surface boundaries are not sharp due to interlayer diffusion, these effects can be modeled by supplemental layers. With these approximations, the sample under study has a given number of layers with parallel boundaries and different complex refractive indices for each layer. Hence, the ellipsometric parameters can be computed for any model with isotropic materials by using Equation (3.4) and (4.1).

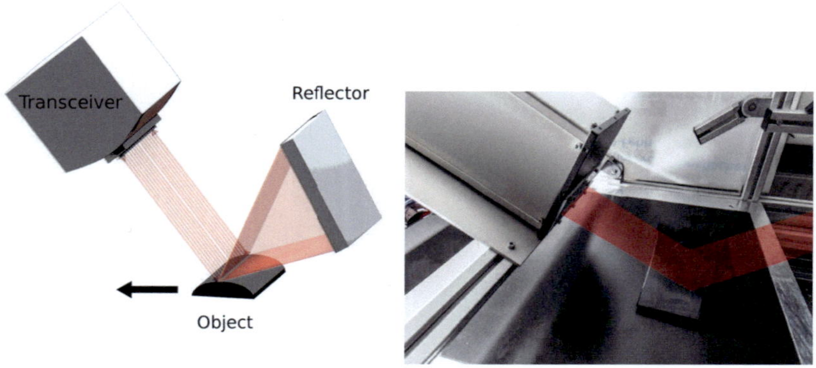

(a) (b)

Figure 5.1: Scheme of the beam path with retroreflection (a) and an image of the ellipsometry scanner (b).

5 Ellipsometry scanner with retroreflection

One difference of the developed ellipsometry scanner to actual spectroscopic ellipsometers is that the polarization state as well as the wavelength of the input beam is fixed. A circularly polarized laser beam is emitted out of the transceiver, reflected off the surface of a moving object and hitting the retroreflector. Because of the retroreflection the beam takes the same light path back into the transceiver with a second reflection at the surface (see Figure 5.1). The use of a retroreflector ensures that the emitted light can be detected even for high deviations of the surface normal, in contrast to the classical ellipsometry configuration. In the transceiver the polarization state is analyzed. In this way, four polarization images are acquired with the azimuthal angles $0°$, $90°$, $45°$ and $135°$ of a linear polarizer.

5.1 Influence of Retroreflection on Psi and Delta

In this section the measurements acquired with an usual ellipsometer are compared to those acquired in a configuration with a retroreflector. It is assumed that the retroreflector does not change the polarization state. There are theoretical indications for that because of the symmetry of the micro glass beads on the surface of the retroreflector. Nevertheless, an experimental examination of possible depolarization effects or anisotropy remains to be performed. Because of the retroreflection it cannot be done with an usual ellipsometer. If the polarization state is not changed by the retroreflector, the following relation holds for the measurements from a conventional ellipsometer Ψ, Δ and those obtained with a retroreflector and a double reflection at the sample surface Ψ', Δ' [NH14]:

$$\tan \Psi' = \tan^2 \Psi,$$
$$\Delta' = 2\Delta,$$
$$\rho' = \rho^2.$$

With the actual prototype the measurement of Ψ' is possible in the full interval $[0°, 90°]$ but Δ' can be only be measured in the interval $[0°, 180°]$. Therefore, Ψ can be recalculated from Ψ' but Δ can only be determined in the interval $[0°, 90°]$. The question is which impact this restriction has on the detectable layer thicknesses and optical constants. The trajectory of Ψ, Δ for a layer on a substrate with fixed refractive indices and variable thicknesses is shown in Figure 5.2(a). As can be seen, with an exception at the singular point, it is possible to compute the refractive index and the layer thickness simultaneously from Ψ, Δ when the periodicity is ignored. This uniqueness will not be given anymore, if the measurements are captured with the ellipsometry scanner as seen in Figure 5.2(b). For every Ψ', Δ' there are two combinations of refractive indices and thicknesses which correspond to the same measurement. As mentioned before, we can determine Δ' only in the interval $[0°, 180°]$. Compared to an ellipsometer which can determine Δ in the whole range, the number of ambiguous solutions in the configuration with a retroreflector is four times higher. Additionally, because the geometry of the surface is unknown there are two more unknown variables θ, ϕ which have to be determined for each pixel, whereas θ is the angle of incidence and ϕ the rotation of the sensor coordinate system with respect to the plane of incidence (see Figure 4.1). If the refractive index of the surface is known and constant on the surface, the thickness and the angle of incidence can be determined as shown in Figure 5.3(a) but it is not possible to also determine ϕ. Therefore, either multiple independent measurements e.g. under different angles of incidence have to be acquired and registered or an additional sensor providing topography data has to be used.

6 Fitting of model parameters

Compared to the number of measurements, usually, only a few parameters are fitted in spectroscopic ellipsometry. These could be the parameters of a predefined

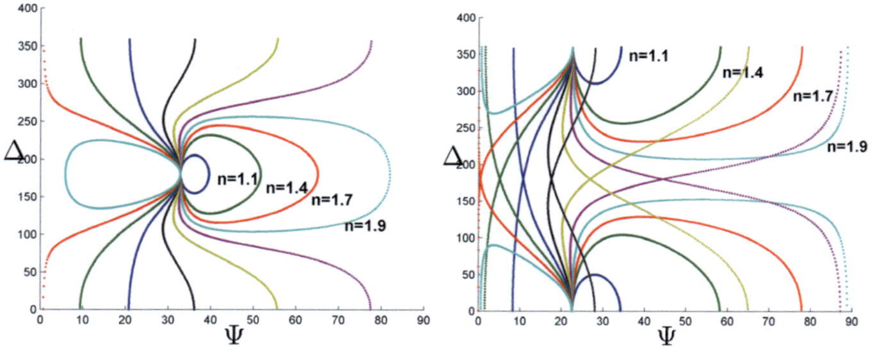

(a) (b)

Figure 5.2: Ψ, Δ trajectory for films with variable thickness and different refractive indices (a). Ψ', Δ' for the same models measured in the configuration with a retroreflector (b).

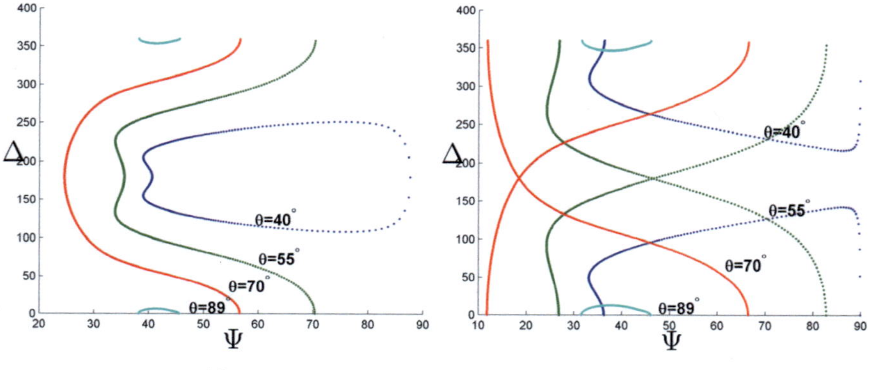

(a) (b)

Figure 5.3: Ψ, Δ trajectory for films with variable thickness and different angles of incidence (a). Ψ', Δ' for the same models measured in the configuration with a retroreflector (b).

oscillator model for the dielectric function, the fraction of known materials for an unknown material modeled by an EMA model or the thickness of roughness layers [TM99]. A problem of this classical approach is, that the materials of the samples of interest are often unknown for our use cases, hence no specific oscillator model can be assumed. One method to overcome this problem is to use point-by-point calculations. When a non-depolarizing, isotropic substrate without a film is present, the refractive index n and the extinction coefficient k can be directly computed from the ellipsometric parameters $\Psi(\lambda)$ and $\Delta(\lambda)$ by Equation (4.2). When there are one or multiple layers on the substrate, the complex refractive indices of the multiple layers cannot be computed from $\Psi(\lambda)$ and $\Delta(\lambda)$ because there are more unknowns than measurements. With VASE this problem does not occur anymore, because we can capture an arbitrary number of measurements at different (known) angles of incidence, although the acquired measurements are not necessarily independent. With the ellipsometry software DeltaPsi2 it is possible to compute the complex refractive index by point-by-point calculations for one material but all other model parameters have to be known. It is neither possible to fit the layer thickness and the refractive index with a point-by-point calculation nor to fit the refractive indices of multiple layers at once. When there is little knowledge about the materials the sample consists of, this functionality is needed. Therefore, an own software framework to provide more flexible computations with VASE measurements is implemented in MATLAB. Like other ellipsometry software frameworks it contains of the following functionalities:

- Computation of Ψ, Δ in a simulation step for a given model consisting of a layer stack with given thicknesses and optical material constants.
- Computation of the goodness of fit as the mean square error (MSE) of the measured Ψ_M, Δ_M and predicted values Ψ_P, Δ_P.
- Updating the model until the goodness of fit reaches a predefined threshold.

The MSE is computed by:

$$\text{MSE} = \frac{1}{\text{\#wavelengts}} \sum_{\lambda} (\Psi_M(\lambda) - \Psi_P(\lambda))^2 + \operatorname{mod}(\Delta_M(\lambda) - \Delta_P(\lambda), 2\pi)^2.$$

For obtaining the complex refractive index of the substrate, no fitting is needed, because Equation (4.2) can be used to compute the refractive index analytically. For obtaining the complex refractive index of the layer for a given thickness, a nonlinear optimization has to be performed. The algorithm used for the nonlinear optimization is differential evolution [1].

[1] Available at http://www.mathworks.com/matlabcentral/fileexchange/18593-differential-evolution

The optical properties of a coated surface with unknown material are determined by first computing the optical properties of the substrate and then fitting the optical properties of the layer. This is an adequate procedure because it is often possible to take an uncoated and a coated sample out of the manufacturing process. Because the layer thickness is also unknown, it must be fitted. One possibility is to fit all model parameters in a high dimensional space at once, which would result in unnecessary function calls of the objective function because of the independence of the refractive indices for different wavelengths. Instead, the fitting of the thickness is implemented as a wrapper around the fitting of the material properties. The wrapper algorithm iterates over thickness values obtained on a coarse grid within the search interval and calls the optimization function for fitting the material properties for given layer thickness. Then, the wrapper algorithm iteratively performs a refinement of the grid while minimizing the search interval of the thickness. The center of new search interval is set at the best thickness value found in the last iteration.

6.1 Numerical Experiment

The first step in testing the accuracy of the proposed fitting algorithm is to compute VASE spectrum measurements from a ground truth model by employing the DeltaPsi2 software and trying to fit the model parameters with the implemented software framework from the simulated measurements. For a classical use case in ellipsometry, a film of silicon dioxide $\mathrm{SiO_2}$ on crystalline silicon $\mathrm{c\text{-}Si}$, measurements for the wavelength range from 440 nm to 1000 nm and for varying angle of incidence from $45°$ to $80°$ were generated. The dispersion formulas for $\mathrm{SiO_2}$ and $\mathrm{c\text{-}Si}$ were taken out of the material database which is part of the DeltaPsi2 software. Two layer thicknesses were analyzed, a 100 nm thick and a 1000 nm thick $\mathrm{SiO_2}$ layer.

After the optical properties of the substrate are computed from the measurements, the refractive index $\underline{n}_2$ of a 100 nm thick $\mathrm{SiO_2}$ layer is fitted. Because the thickness is small, there are not many oscillations of Ψ, Δ when $\underline{n}_2$ varies, hence there is a low number of local minima, which results in a good fit (MSE=0.0002). The fit for the refractive index is shown in Figure 6.1(a), while the ground truth is blue and the fitted values are green. In Figure 6.1(b) the MSE is shown as a heat map when the refractive index varies ($\lambda = 620$ nm). Two local minima exist at $\underline{n}_2 = 1.46 - 0i$ and at $\underline{n}_2 = 1 - 2i$. When a film of 1000 nm is present, the fit is not good (MSE=288.1) because the algorithm often ends up in local minima which is visible at the outliers in Figure 6.2(a). At $k = 0$ it is also visible that the MSE

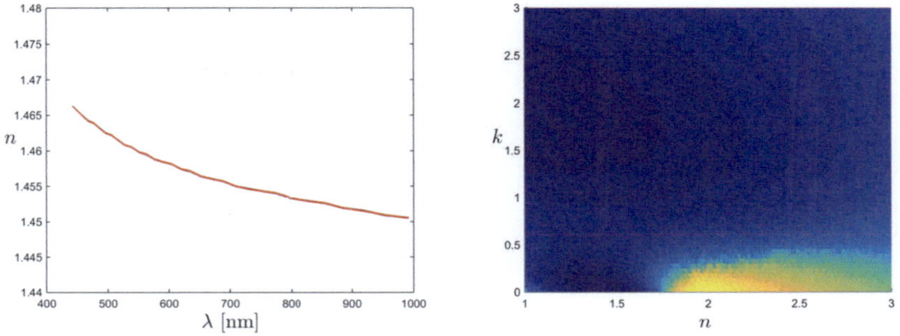

(a) (b)

Figure 6.1: In (a) the fitting result of the refractive index of a 100 nm thick film is shown. In (b) a heat map of the MSE for $\underline{n}_2$ is depicted ($\lambda = 620$ nm).

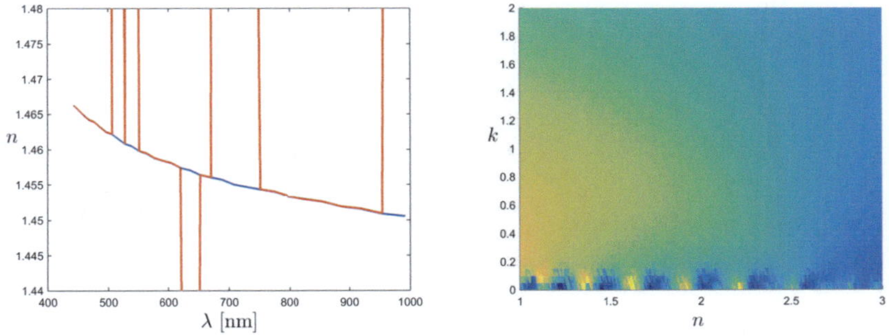

(a) (b)

Figure 6.2: In (a) the fitting result of the refractive index of a 1000 nm thick film is shown. In (b) a heat map of the MSE for $\underline{n}_2$ is depicted ($\lambda = 620$ nm).

oscillates (see Figure 6.2(b)) which results in many local minima and complicates the fitting procedure.

The result of the layer thickness obtained with the wrapper algorithm is shown in Figure 6.3. For every thickness value set by the wrapper algorithm in each iteration, the corresponding MSE value computed by the differential evolution fitting algorithm is shown in the figure. If the layer thickness is 100 nm, the fitted thickness with the wrapper algorithm is 100.1 nm (MSE=0.021). If it is 1000 nm, the fitted thickness is 1001 nm (MSE=81.1). In both cases it seems that the function

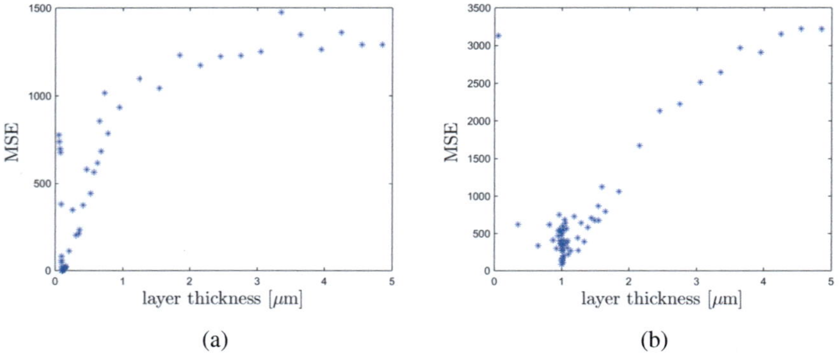

Figure 6.3: Fitting results of the wrapper optimization algorithm for a 100 nm (a) and a 1000 nm (b) thick layer.

for fitting the optical material properties often ended up in local minima because of the high variance of the MSE for similar thickness values.

7 Summary and Outlook

In this article, several problems arising in the context of applying ellipsometry on curved surfaces and possible applications were discussed. The main focus lies on samples with one or two layers which are up to several μm thick. An optimization technique was proposed to determine the optical constants via VASE. In a simulation the thickness as well as the optical constants could be determined for a 100 nm or a 1000 nm thick layer. Because of many oscillations of the objective function at thick layers, the fitting often ends up in a local minimum. Further analysis needs to be performed, to verify if the envelope of the oscillations could be used to localize the region of the global optimum. Because the dimension of the search space is quite low it is probably possible to improve the fitting to find the global optimum. If the estimation of the optical properties could be improved, the next step would be to check if the optical constants of the two layers could be fitted simultaneously without a separate measurement of the substrate.

Some problems related to point-by-point calculations could be avoided using B-splines to represent the dielectric function. This is a compromise between the usage of dispersion models and point-by-point calculations. Dispersion models are physically correct but unpractical to use with unknown materials because the oscillator type and starting parameters have to be chosen. Dielectric functions obtained by point-by-point calculations are prone to sensor noise, possess discontinuities, and neglect the Kramers-Kronig consistency. In [JH08] the usage of Kramers-Kronig consistent basis functions based on B-Splines is proposed. This could be used in the fitting procedure to avoid the mentioned problems resulting from point-by-point calculations.

Bibliography

[BPLF12] Jürgen Beyerer, Fernando Puente León, and Christian Frese. *Automatische Sichtprüfung: Grundlagen, Methoden und Praxis der Bildgewinnung und Bildauswertung*. SpringerLink : Bücher. Springer, Berlin and Heidelberg, 2012.

[FGS+95] H. Fu, T. Goodman, S. Sugaya, J. K. Erwin, and M. Mansuripur. Retroreflecting ellipsometer for measuring the birefringence of optical disk substrates. *Applied optics*, 34(1):31–39, 1995.

[Fra] Fraunhofer-Gesellschaft zur Förderung der angewandten Forschung e.V. Vorrichtung und Verfahren zur optischen Charakterisierung von Materialien / Apparatus and method for optically characterizing materials. Patents EP11760701.0 (09.09.2011), DE 10 2010 046 438.4-52 (29.03.2012), WO 2012/038036 A1 (29.03.2012), US-2013-0222803-A1 (29.08.2013).

[JH08] Blaine Johs and Jeffrey S. Hale. Dielectric function representation by B-splines. *physica status solidi (a)*, 205(4):715–719, 2008.

[NH14] Christian Negara and Matthias Hartrumpf. Ellipsometrie an gekrümmten Oberflächen. In Fernando Puente León, editor, *Forum Bildverarbeitung 2014*, pages 227–238, Karlsruhe, 2014. KIT Scientific Publishing.

[NR02] Ulrich Neuschaefer-Rube, editor. *Optische Oberflächenmesstechnik für Topografie und Material*, volume 953 of *Fortschritt-Berichte VDI Reihe 8, Meß-, Steuerungs- und Regelungstechnik*. VDI-Verl., Düsseldorf, 2002.

[TM99] Harland G. Tompkins and William A. McGahan. *Spectroscopic ellipsometry and reflectometry: A user's guide*. Wiley, New York, 1999.

Towards smooth generic camera calibration

Alexey Pak

Vision and Fusion Laboratory
Institute for Anthropomatics
Karlsruhe Institute of Technology (KIT), Germany
alexey.pak@ies.uni-karlsruhe.de

Technical Report IES-2014-06

Abstract: In the common approach to the generic camera calibration (GCC), one uses dense ray coding (with e.g. active grids displayed on an LCD screen) in order to find the ray origin and direction for each camera pixel independently. While applicable to many types of imaging sensors, the GCC fails to describe the local differential properties of ray bundles that are important in e.g. studying the geometry of infinitesimal scene changes via optical flow. In this report, we investigate the alternative approach to the GCC where the camera ray origins and directions are assumed to be differentiable functions of the sensor position. In particular, we present a novel calibration technique based on finite element method that unites the ray update and bundle adjustment stages of the common GCC and accommodates arbitrary anisotropic coding uncertainties and non-planar coding surfaces. The accuracy and the stability of the resulting smooth generic camera calibration (sGCC) algorithm are verified based on some non-trivial synthetic examples.

1 Introduction

The geometric camera model is a mapping $(u, v) \to \{\vec{o}_c, \vec{r}_c\}$ that assigns to each sensor pixel with cooridnates (u, v) a three-dimensional ray that originates in point $\vec{o}_c$ and is directed along the vector $\vec{r}_c$ (both defined in the local camera's system of coordinates). It is assumed that any point on that ray projects to the same pixel[1].

The simplest model that is widely adopted in computer graphics and in computer vision is a pinhole camera. It assumes a single projection center $\vec{o}_c$ for all pixels and some parameterization of $\vec{r}_c(u, v)$ which in the simplest case is linear:

$$\vec{o}_c(u, v) = (0, 0, 0)^T, \;\; \vec{r}_c(u, v) = (a_1 u + a_2 v, a_3 u + a_4 v, 1)^T. \qquad (1.1)$$

[1] In this report we ignore any finite sharpness effects.

The coefficients a_1, ..., a_4 may describe the "anisotropic magnification" and the "skewness" of the camera. (From here on, we assume that the center of the sensor is at $(u, v) = (0, 0)$.) Note that provided the coefficients a_1, ..., a_4 and the extrinsic camera parameters, one can easily find the inverse mapping that determines a sensor projection for any given 3D point.

When high-precision results are needed and/or when complex cameras and lenses are used, the linear pinhole model becomes too inaccurate and leads to systematic errors both in image generation and exploitation. One possible way to fix Eq. (1.1) is to introduce a few higher-order polynomial corrections into the second equation.

The calibration for the linear model as well as for the model with a few correction terms can be performed with the convenient algorithm developed by Zhang [Zha00] that is implemented e.g. in the OpenCV library [Bra00]. One needs only a few images of a flat static textured pattern (such as a checkerboard) taken from at least three different camera poses. The algorithm uses a sparse subset of features recognizable in all images (e.g. corners) in order to determine the camera poses and the model parameters.

However, even the corrected pinole model cannot accurately describe cameras with multiple projection centers or those with a wide-angle ($> 180^\circ$) field of view. It is also insufficiently accurate for the metrological tasks where more higher-order corrections need to be compensated for, than what is allowed by a fixed-order model. The more accurate model-independent technique of the generic camera calibration (GCC) [SR03, RSL05] attempts to produce a large look-up table with two vectors $\{\vec{o}_c[i], \vec{r}_c[i]\}$ per each camera pixel i. This model allows one to describe different visual sensors, including arbitrary multi-camera or catadioptric systems; it is also used in precision metrology (see e.g. [RLBB14] and references therein).

Unfortunately, the look-up table concept is notoriously inconvenient for the solution of the inverse problem. Indeed, given a 3D point, one needs to search the entire table for the "respective" pixel that minimizes the re-projection error. The lack of the neighborhood information for each pixel also complicates the analysis of the 3D motion that results in small image displacements over the sensor. Since the pixel coordinates u and v are not explicitly used, the derivatives such as $\partial\vec{o}_c/\partial u$ cannot be evaluated efficiently. Even if all pixels in some neighborhood have been found, the independent processing of camera pixels in the GCC algorithm leads to uncorrelated noise in $\vec{o}_c[i]$ and $\vec{r}_c[i]$ that necessitates the use of higher-order schemes to evaluate the partial derivatives numerically.

In practical implementation, the GCC requires a dense map of correspondences that cannot be obtained with static patterns. Instead, one uses active screens that project coding patterns in synchronization with the camera. For each camera pose, the screen displays a series of patterns and the camera records images so that the

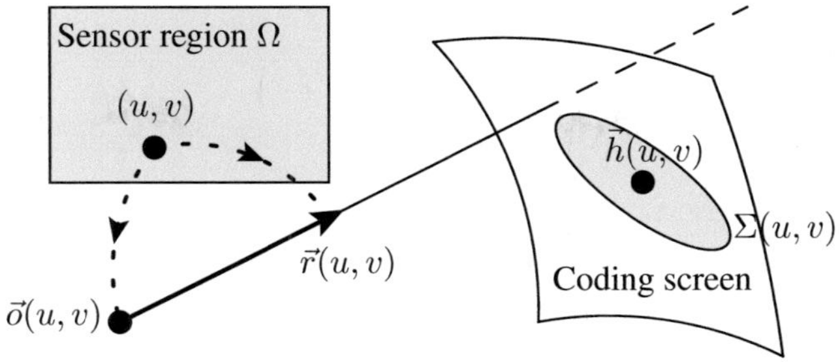

Figure 2.1: Geometry of camera calibration with active coding screen

3D position of the screen pixel that projects to a camera pixel can be decoded from the unique series of the recorded values.

In this report we present the formulation of the variation of the GCC that we call smooth GCC (sGCC) that uses the same input data as the regular GCC in order to recover the smooth functions $\vec{o}_c(u, v)$ and $\vec{r}_c(u, v)$ that alleviate the problems outlined above.

2 Single ray consistency metric

In the calibration setup shown in Fig. 2.1 we consider one camera ray that hits the known arbitrary active coding surface. The global and the camera frames are related via translation vector $\vec{t}$ and the rotation matrix R (six parameter in total). In the camera's own frame, the ray origin is $\vec{o}_c(u, v)$ and its direction is $\vec{r}_c(u, v)$ where $(u, v) \in \Omega$ denote the corresponding sensor position within the limits of some region Ω. For the purpose of further discussion we assume that the coordinates u and v are continuous and that the derivatives of $\vec{o}_c(u, v)$ and $\vec{r}_c(u, v)$ are finite in every point inside Ω.

The respective coding point $\vec{h}(u, v)$ on the screen can only be determined with some finite accuracy. Typically, if a flat LCD screen is used, the lateral uncertainty is not much better than its pixel size. The depth, however, is usually known more accurately (it may e.g. be due to the non-planarity of the screen and the refraction of light in the glass). We thus may only establish the position of the coding point up to some uncertainty ellisoid around $\vec{h}$ characterized by the covariance matrix $\Sigma(u, v)$. The latter is either known a priori or can be determined directly from the coding data and the photometric parameters of the camera [FPT12].

The agreement of the calibrated camera ray with the decoded screen position must be characterized with respect to this ellipsoid. Combining all the pieces together, we suggest the following scalar ray consistency metric:

$$\Delta = \min_{\alpha} \left(\vec{o} + \alpha\vec{r} - \vec{h}\right)^T \cdot \Sigma^{-1} \cdot \left(\vec{o} + \alpha\vec{r} - \vec{h}\right), \tag{2.1}$$

where the ray origin and the direction in global frame are given by $\vec{o} = \vec{t} + R \cdot \vec{o}_c$ and $\vec{r} = R \cdot \vec{r}_c$ and we suppressed the arguments (u, v) everywhere for brevity.

The minimum in Eq. (2.1) can be found in closed form. Indeed, every symmetric positive-definite matrix Σ can be decomposed as $\Sigma^{-1} = \Lambda^T \cdot \Lambda$, and we find

$$\Delta = \vec{\delta}^{\,T} \cdot \vec{\delta} \text{ with } \vec{\delta} = \vec{o}\,' - \vec{r}\,' \frac{\left(\vec{r}\,'^T \cdot \vec{o}\,'\right)}{\left(\vec{r}\,'^T \cdot \vec{r}\,'\right)} \tag{2.2}$$

$$\text{where } \vec{o}\,' = \Lambda \cdot \left(\vec{o} - \vec{h}\right) \text{ and } \vec{r}\,' = \Lambda \cdot \vec{r}.$$

In particular, if $\Lambda = I$, then the metric of Eq. (2.2) is equivalent to the common Euclidean distance between the line and the point $\vec{h}$ in 3D.

It shoud be noted that the ray definition above is not unique. Indeed, any change $\vec{o}_c \to \vec{o}_c + \alpha\vec{r}_c$ or $\vec{r}_c \to \beta\vec{r}_c$ for any α and β results in the identical imaging geometry and leaves Δ invariant. Such trivial freedom can be removed by introducing two additional constraints which in general may depend on the camera type. In what follows, we limit ourselves with single-sensor cameras whose field of view is less than $180°$. In this case, one can use the following simple constraints:

$$(\vec{o}_c(u, v))_3 = 0 \text{ and } (\vec{r}_c(u, v))_3 = 1 \; \forall (u, v) \in \Omega. \tag{2.3}$$

3 Calibration as optimization problem

The ideal calibration means that $\Delta(u, v)$ vanishes over the entire sensor. Indeed, if the decoded data are available for three or more camera poses and we neglect the inter-pixel correlations, the regular GCC may determine $\vec{o}_c(u_i, v_i)$ and $\vec{r}_c(u_i, v_i)$ for all sensor pixels $i = 1, ..., N$ without any relation to the decoding error $\Sigma(u, v)$. However, the independently found origins and directions will likely contain high-frequency noise that may mask any real differential behaviour of these functions.

Instead, in the suggested sGCC framework we attempt to find *smooth* functions $\vec{o}_c(u, v)$ and $\vec{r}_c(u, v)$ that minimize the discrepancy $\Delta(u, v)$ *integrated over the sensor*. The smoothness of these functions is defined a priori and provides the separation between the variations perceived as noise and those assumed to be instrinsic features of the camera.

The practical implementation is formulated in terms of the finite element method (FEM) as follows. First, we search for the calibration functions as linear combinations of smooth kernels $\psi_i(u,v)$, $i = 1, ..., P$. Their "size" and smoothness control the properties of the solution. The noise in Δ is filtered out by the convolution with some smooth probe functions $\phi_k(u,v)$, $k = 1, ..., M$. The entire problem then is discretized. For a single camera pose, we have:

$$\vec{o}_c\left(u, v|\vec{C}\right) = \sum_{i=1}^{P} \left(c_i^{(o1)}\psi_i(u,v), c_i^{(o2)}\psi_i(u,v), c_i^{(o3)}\psi_i(u,v)\right)^T, \tag{3.1}$$

$$\vec{r}_c\left(u, v|\vec{C}\right) = \sum_{i=1}^{P} \left(c_i^{(r1)}\psi_i(u,v), c_i^{(r2)}\psi_i(u,v), c_i^{(r3)}\psi_i(u,v)\right)^T,$$

$$\vec{C}^* = \operatorname{argmin}_{\vec{C}} \left\{\sum_{k=1}^{M} \|\vec{D}_k\|^2\right\}, \quad \vec{D}_k = \int_{\Omega} \phi_k(u,v)\, \vec{\delta}\left(u, v|\vec{C}\right) du\, dv,$$

where $\vec{\delta}\left(u, v|\vec{C}\right)$ is defined in Eq. 2.2 (trivially adapted for the given camera ray parameterization), $\vec{C} = \left(\vec{c}^{\,(o1)}, \vec{c}^{\,(o2)}, \vec{c}^{\,(o3)}, \vec{c}^{\,(r1)}, \vec{c}^{\,(r2)}, \vec{c}^{\,(r3)}, \vec{t}, \vec{\theta}\right)^T$ is the vector of concatenated model parameters, including the camera translation $\vec{t}$ and the three Euler angles $\vec{\theta}$ that determine the camera rotation matrix R.

Per se, Eq. (3.1) does not lead to a unique solution. First, as in the regular GCC, one needs data from several independent camera poses. The respective changes to the metric are straightforward, each pose adding six parameters to $\vec{C}$ and $3M$ terms to the sum under argmin. Second, we need to enforce the uniqueness conditions Eq. (2.3). Finally, we must fix the camera position and the orientation with respect to the view rays. We again resort to the simplest suitable conditions:

$$\vec{o}_c(0,0) = (0,0,0)^T, \ \vec{r}_c(0,0) = (0,0,1)^T, \text{ and } \frac{\partial(\vec{r}_c)_2}{\partial u}(0,0) = 0.$$

This fixes all six degrees of freedom of the camera in its own frame with respect to the ray bundle near the central pixel $(0,0)$.

Due to the linearity of $\vec{o}_c$ and $\vec{r}_c$ with respect to the coefficients $\vec{c}^{\,(oi)}$ and $\vec{c}^{\,(ri)}$, all these constraints can be succintly represented in matrix form as $A \cdot \vec{C} = \vec{b}$. We thus recognize Eq. (3.1) as a constrained non-linear least squares problem which can be efficiently solved by iterative methods.

For the practical implementation, we chose to define the kernel functions ψ_i and probe functions ϕ_k as the uniform cubic B-splines with control points on a regular

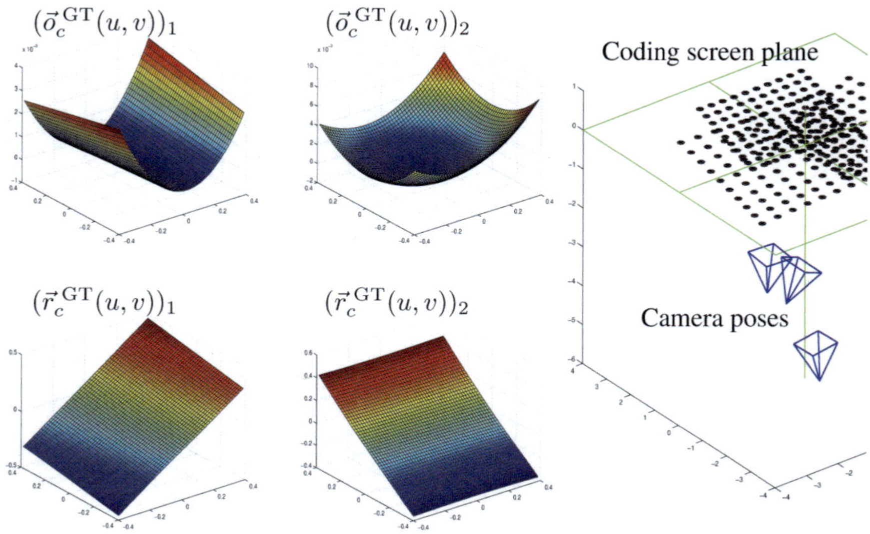

Figure 3.1: Ground truth calibration functions $\vec{o}_c^{\,\mathrm{GT}}(u,v)$ and $\vec{r}_c^{\,\mathrm{GT}}(u,v)$, actual camera poses and a selection of decoded screen points (black spots represent the uncertainty ellipsoids exaggerated by a factor of ten).

rectangular mesh in (u,v)-space. In order to solve to the optimization problem, we used the `levmar` library [Lou04].

With such choices, the dimensionality of the problem is controlled by the mesh dimensions. For instance, a mesh of 4×4 finite elements has 49 basic functions, which for three poses translates to 312 parameters in $\vec{C}$. After accounting for the linear constraints, 209 independent degrees of freedom are left, with the least squares solution to be found in 441-dimensional space (all components of $\vec{\delta}$ are considered separately). Such problem can only be efficiently solved if the respective Jacobian matrix is known. Fortunately, all components of Eq. (3.1) are known analytically and the respective derivatives $\partial\vec{D}_k/\partial(\vec{C})_j$ can be easily found manually or using the automated differentiation techniques.

4 Numerical experiment

In order to verify the feasibility and the correctness of the sGCC algorithm, we have carried out the following synthetic experiment. For some pre-defined non-trivial functions $\vec{o}_c^{\,\mathrm{GT}}(u,v)$ and $\vec{r}_c^{\,\mathrm{GT}}(u,v)$ and the three camera poses (Fig. 3.1)

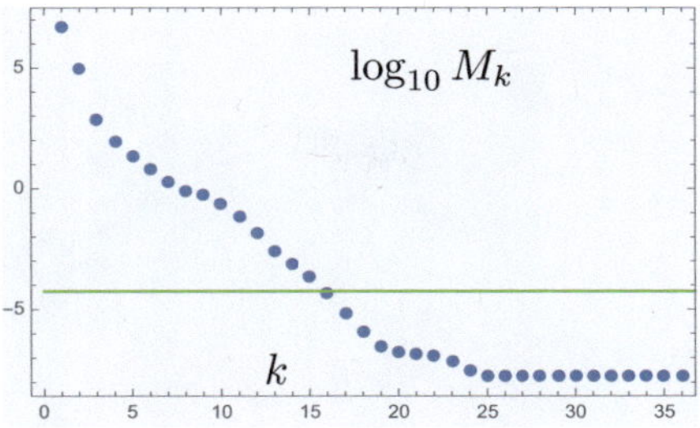

Figure 4.1: The optimization metric during the run, k is the iteration. The green line corresponds to the direct fit of splines to the ground truth functions.

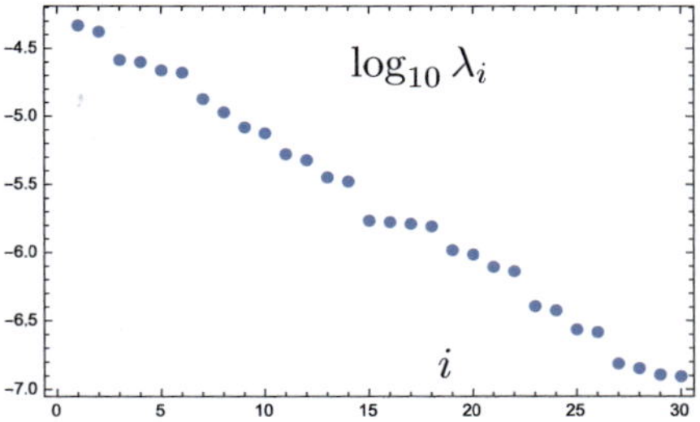

Figure 4.2: The largest eigenvalues of the covariance matrix estimated during the optimization.

we have performed the camera calibration using a 4×4 mesh in a window $(u, v) \in \Omega = [-0.4, 0.4]^2$. The typical distance from the camera to the screen was 4 units, the typical variation of $\vec{o}_c$ was 10^{-3} units, and the $\vec{r}_c$ was a smooth perturbation of order 10^{-3} units on top of a linear pinhole camera.

In order to initialize the numerical optimization, we assumed that the results of a simpler calibration (e.g., with the Zhang's method) were available. In particular, we initialize the intrinsic parameters with some perfect pinhole model, and choose the starting camera positions to deviate by about 0.1 units from the actual points. The starting camera orientations we also inaccurate by about 0.1 radians.

The 40 optimization iterations took about twenty minutes on a laptop (Intel Core i7 CPU, one thread). The optimization converged relatively fast (in about 25 iterations), the corresponding change in the optimization metric of Eq. (3.1) is shown in Fig. 4.1. It is remarkable that the found optimum provides a three orders of magnitude smaller metric value than the best fit of splines directly to the ground truth functions (the respective value denoted by the green line in Fig. 4.1).

The resulting accuracy of the intrinsic calibration functions $\vec{o}_c^{\,*}$ and $\vec{r}_c^{\,*}$ is of the order of 10^{-6} to 10^{-4} units (Fig. 4.3). The final camera position accuracy is about 10^{-4} units, and the error in its orientation is of the order of 10^{-6} radians.

In order to study the shape of the optimization function near the optimum, we also computed a few largest eigenvalues of the covariance matrix estimated by `levmar` (Fig. 4.2). The lack of large "steps" in the magnitudes of eigenvalues can be considered the sign of the "uniqueness" of the found solution.

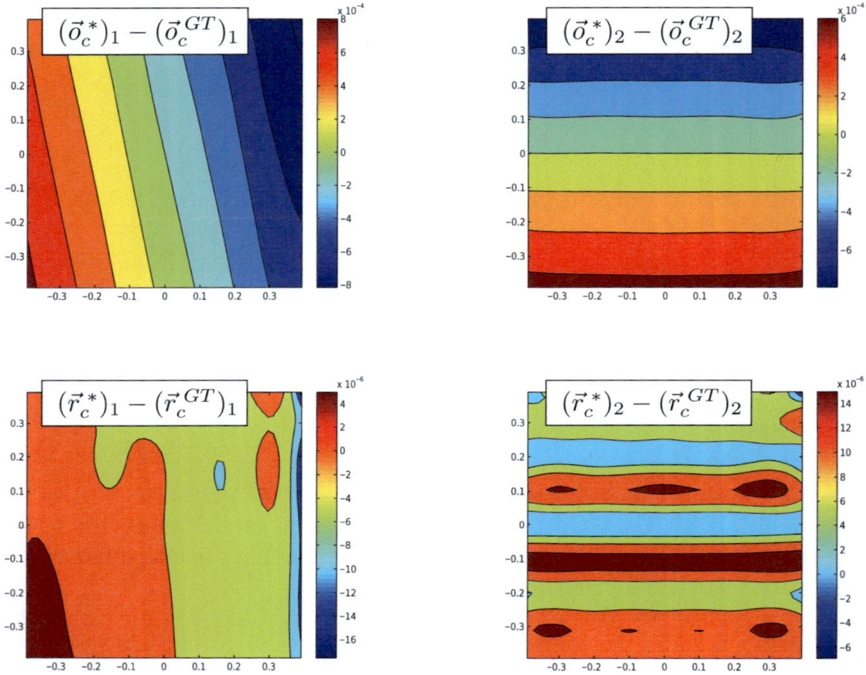

Figure 4.3: Reconstruction errors in calibration functions

Of course, one synthetic experiment is not a decisive argument for the method, and a more elaborate investigation is necessary. We consider the present results encouraging and expect similar behaviour in further synthetic and real experiments.

5 Summary

In this report we suggested a novel model-independent camera calibration algorithm (sGCC) suitable for the precision simulation and computer vision applications. We presented the theoretical background and the first numerical results characterizing the FEM-based implementation of the method for "traditional" cameras. In a synthetic experiment, the method has been able to reproduce a non-trivial intrinsic geometry of a camera together with its extrinsic parameters. The achieved re-projection error is 1000 times smaller than that when the calibrated functions are directly fitted to the ground truth. The solution is shown to be numerically stable and non-ambiguous.

The present report does not specify how exactly the sGCC simplifies the inverse (projection) problem. We note here that based on the sGCC results, it is possible to find the locally "best fitting" pinhole camera. Due to the differentiability of the calibration functions, this can be done in closed form (the details are to be presented in further publications). Iteratively projecting the point to those local pihnole cameras, one can find the projection pixel with an any accuracy.

In the future we plan to study the robustness of the sGCC with respect to noise and determine the applicability limits of the technique. We also plan to develop a practical calibration toolbox and study the real and simulated cameras under various conditions in order to compare sGCC against the existing methods.

Bibliography

[Bra00] G. Bradski. The OpenCV library. *Dr. Dobb's Journal of Software Tools*, 2000.

[FPT12] Marc Fischer, Marcus Petz, and Rainer Tutsch. Vorhersage des Phasenrauschens in optischen Messsystemen mit strukturierter Beleuchtung. *Technisches Messen*, 79:451–458, 2012.

[Lou04] M. I. A. Lourakis. levmar: Levenberg-marquardt nonlinear least squares algorithms in C/C++. [web page] `http://www.ics.forth.gr/~lourakis/levmar/`, 2004. [Accessed on 13 Nov 2014].

[RLBB14] T. Reh, W. Li, Jan Burke, and R. B. Bergmann. Improving the Generic Camera Calibration technique by an extended model of calibration display. *J. Europ. Opt. Soc. Rap. Public.*, 9:14044, 2014.

[RSL05] S. Ramalingam, Peter Sturm, and S. K. Lodha. Theory and experiments towards complete generic calibration. Technical Report 5562, INRIA, 2005.

[SR03] Peter Sturm and Srikumar Ramalingam. A generic calibration concept - theory and algorithms. Research Report 5058, INRIA, 2003.

[Zha00] Z. Zhang. A flexible new technique for camera calibration. *IEEE Trans. Pattern Anal. Machine Intell.*, 22:1330–1334, 2000.

Distributed Constrained Optimization over Constrained Communication Topologies

Julius Pfrommer

Vision and Fusion Laboratory
Institute for Anthropomatics
Karlsruhe Institute of Technology (KIT), Germany
julius.pfrommer@kit.edu

Technical Report IES-2014-07

Abstract: The Max-Sum algorithm, an instance of the Generalized Distributive Law family, is known to solve Distributed Constraint Optimization Problems (DCOP) where the summed utility functions of interacting agents are maximized. However, Max-Sum relies on available communication channels between all agents that partake in a utility function. We present a generalization of Max-Sum that solves DCOP exactly in situations where the communication network layout does not match the agents' utility inter-dependencies.

1 Introduction

In Distributed Constraint Optimization (DCOP), a set of agents (each represented by a variable that represents his action, choosen from a finite domain) coordinates their actions in order to maximize the summed utility the agents experience. In this work we built upon the well-known Max-Sum algorithm, a member of the Generalized Distributive Law (GDL) family of message passing schemes [AM00] [KFL01]. Max-Sum is widely used for DCOP [PF05] [KV06], however, message-passing with Max-Sum is only guaranteed to converge to a maximum assignment if the utility inter-dependencies of the agents form a tree-graph. Here, we present a generalization of Max-Sum that can infer the exact max-marginals in deterministic time on DCOP instances where

1. not all (inter-dependent) agents can exchange messages, but the communication graph is still connected
2. agent inter-dependencies form loops.

Existing DCOP algorithms can be roughly classified into search based [MSTY05], local-search based [MTB+04] and inference based [PF05] methods. Our approach falls into the inference based class of algorithms. It is different from DCOP in settings where communication is limited/expensive [FRPJ08] [PGCMRA11] as we constrain the the availability of communication channels and not only the throughput. It also differs from exact and approximate inference on junction trees for DCOP [BM10] [VRAC11]. Our method requires no graph triangulation and grouping of agents into a tree-like hypergraph. Instead, we cut communication links between interacting agents until the remaining graph forms a tree. The messages exchanged between agents are adapted, so that local utility information is propagated within the relevant portions of the graph only. This leads to a very natural handling of situations where the communication topology ist constrained.

The paper is organized as follows. We give an overview on the original Max-Sum algorithm in Section 2. In Section 3, we introduce Max-Sum with Remote Neighbours. The performance of our approach is evaluated on an example scenario in Section 4. The paper concludes in Section 5 with a discussion of the results and some pointers for future research.

2 The Max-Sum Algorithm

Let V be a set of variables $i \in V$, each defined on a finite domain $\mathcal{X}_i$. The goal is to maximize some function f where $\mathcal{X} = \prod_{i \in V} \mathcal{X}_i,\ f : \mathcal{X} \to \mathbb{R}_{-\infty}$. The codomain $\mathbb{R}_{-\infty} = \mathbb{R} \cup \{-\infty\}$ makes complex constraints easier to handle algorithmically. That is, if x is constrained to lie in some set $\tilde{\mathcal{X}} \subset \mathcal{X}$, we define $\forall x \notin \tilde{\mathcal{X}}, f(x) = -\infty$ and keep the cartesian product of the variable domains $\mathcal{X}_i$ as the domain of f. This leads to the same maximum solution, provided that $\sup_{x \in \tilde{\mathcal{X}}} f(x) > -\infty$. The trivial approach to enumerate all possible solutions

$$x^* = \arg\max_{x \in \mathcal{X}} f(x)$$

obviously scales exponentially in the number of variables and must fail even for modest problem sizes. Instead, we exploit the structure of the specific f at hand. Assume that f is a sum of functions ψ_α, called *factors*, each of which depends only on a subset of the variables $\alpha \in 2^V$. The set of all factors is $A \subset 2^V$:

$$f(x) = \sum_{\alpha \in A} \psi_\alpha(x_\alpha), \quad x_\alpha \in \prod_{i \in \alpha} \mathcal{X}_i,\ \forall i \in \alpha, (x_\alpha)_i = x_i$$

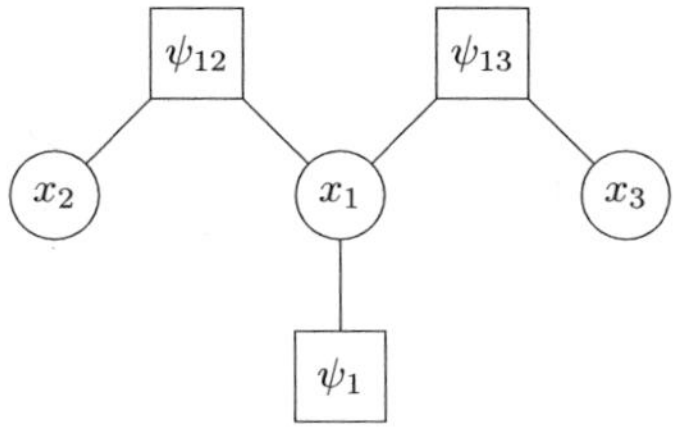

Figure 2.1: Example factor graph corresponding to $f(x_1, x_2, x_3) = \psi_1(x_1) + \psi_{12}(x_1, x_2) + \psi_{13}(x_1, x_3)$. By convention, variable nodes are represented as circles and factor nodes as squares.

This decomposition of f can be represented as a bipartite undirected *factor-graph* $G = (V, A, E)$. See [KFL01] and Fig. 2.1 for an example of a factor graph. Edges (i, α) indicate that the factor ψ_α depends on the variable i. Even though G is undirected, let E contain a pair of directed edges $e = (\underline{e}, \overline{e})$ for every factor-variable relationship to denote directed communication when it occurs. W.l.o.g., assume G to be connected. If that is not the case, G is made up of independent subgraphs $G_k = (V_k, A_k, E_k)$. Since there are no edges (i, α) between subgraphs with $i \in V_k,\ \alpha \in A_{k'}$ for $k \neq k'$, optimizing f reduces to solving

$$x_k^* = \arg\max_{x_k \in \mathcal{X}_k} \sum_{\alpha \in A_k} \psi_\alpha(x_\alpha), \quad \mathcal{X}_k = \prod_{i \in V_k} \mathcal{X}_i$$

independently for each subgraph k, to which the techniques for connected graphs apply.

The Max-Sum algorithm is an instance of the Generalized Distributive Law (GDL) family of algorithms used for solving inference problems that can be stated in terms of a factor graph [KFL01]. GDL is defined on commutative semirings. Max-Sum, according to the problem statement in the beginning of this section, assumes the specific ring $(+, 0, \max, -\infty)$, taking $+$ as the operator for combining *factorisations* and $\max$ as the operator for the *marginalisation* of variables with their respective identity element. Other commutative semirings are widely used as well, e.g. for probabilistic reasoning, but are not discussed here.

Max-Sum relies on communication channels between the variable and factor nodes over which they exchange message-functions $m : \mathcal{X}_i \to \mathbb{R}_{-\infty}$ where the variable i is either the sending or the receiving variable node[1]. Variable nodes i send messages to the factor nodes in their neighborhoud $N(i) = \{\alpha : (i, \alpha) \in E\}$ and

[1]Here, they represent a mapping from a discrete domain to a scalar value which can be trivially encoded as a table for communication.

factor nodes send messages to the $i \in \alpha$. Further, assume discrete time periods t in which every node exchanges messages with all of its neighbours. Often times the messages are initialized to zero in t_0. Other initializations may have better convergence properties, but are not discussed here.

$$
\begin{aligned}
m^{t_0}_{i\to\alpha}(x_i) &= m^{t_0}_{\alpha\to i}(x_i) = 0 \\
m^{t}_{i\to\alpha}(x_i) &= \kappa + \sum_{\beta\in N(i)\setminus\{\alpha\}} m^{t-1}_{\beta\to i}(x_i) \\
m^{t}_{\alpha\to i}(x_i) &= \kappa + \max_{x_{\alpha\setminus\{i\}}} \left[\psi_\alpha(x_\alpha) + \sum_{j\in\alpha\setminus\{i\}} m^{t-1}_{j\to\alpha}(x_j)\right]
\end{aligned}
\tag{2.1a}
$$

Maximizing over $x_{\alpha\setminus\{i\}}$ in (2.1a) should be read as maximizing over $x_\alpha \in \prod_{l\in\alpha}\mathcal{X}_l,\ (x_\alpha)_i = x_i$ where the component of x_α related to variable i is fixed to x_i. When summing over $j \in \alpha \setminus \{i\}$, we denote the component of x_α related to variable j as x_j. The normalisation constant κ is selected for every message so that the message-function is zero for the first element in the domain of the message. The normalisation is required for convergence in loopy graphs, even though it does not guarantee convergence. Otherwise, the values of the exchanged messages can grow or diminish undefinitely. Note that the normalisation does not change the assignments selected during maximization since all choices are over- or underestimated by the same amount. Normalisation does however prevent the computation of the true marginals at the nodes with local information only.

If G is a tree-like factor graph without loops, the exchanged messages converge after completing a forwards/backwards schedule. This schedule says that nodes can only send messages to a neighbour if they have received messages from all other neighbours. Consequently, the schedule starts at the leaf nodes, propagates throughout the tree and ends when all leaf nodes have received a message themselves. Then, the sum of the messages that a variable node i has received is the max-marginal of i on the original function f (up to normalization hat will not change the max assignment computed via the max-marginal). For a proof of this, see Proposition 2 for the proposed Max-Sum with Remote Neighbours, of which, by Proposition 3, the original Max-Sum algorithm is a special case. In loopy graphs, a forward/backwards schedule obviously cannot work. Instead, nodes can send messages asynchronously at any time. For example, every node sends in every period t a message to every neighbour. Randomized schedules are also commonly used in distributed settings. There are no guarantuees for convergence on loopy graph. But if Max-Sum converges, then its solution is a local minima of the Bethe free energy [YFW05] and therefore often useful in practice.

3 Max-Sum with Remote Neighbours

Let $G = (V, A, E)$ be a loopy factor graph. We remove edges until $G' = (V, A, E')$ with $E' \subset E$ forms a tree-graph but is still connected. Now, some factors in A depend on a variable to which they have no edge in the graph. We call these the *remote neighbours* of the factor. The set of both direct and remote neighbours of a factor node is $\tilde{N}(\alpha)$ and $\tilde{N}(i)$ for a variable node. In settings where variables represent agents and their utilities, it is natural to have factors that depend on the choices of several agents, but with a utility that is "local" to a single agent. In that case, we split the relevant factor $\alpha \in A$ into α^i, such that $\psi_\alpha(x_\alpha) = \sum_{i\in\alpha} \psi_{\alpha^i}(x_\alpha)$. The superscript denotes the variable to which the split factor has a direct connection in the graph. See Fig. 3.1 for example transformations.

Recall that there is a pair of directed edges $e \in E'$ for all neighborhood relations in G'. Since G' is a tree-graph, removing any edge would divide the tree into two independent subgraphs. We denote the subgraph that is implicitly "on the side" of the sending node $\underline{e}$ as $G'_{\underline{e}}$. Since remote neighbours can only be reached by relaying messages over multiple hops, the rules by which variables are marginalized out in the messages need to be adapted. For this, we introduce *extended messages*

$$\tilde{m}_e = \langle \tilde{V}_e, (c_{e,i}, |\tilde{N}(i)|)_{i\in\tilde{V}_e}, \bar{m}_e \rangle \, .$$

The time-index is omitted for extended messages since Max-Sum with Remote Neighbours is intended only for a forwards/backwards pass schedule on tree-graphs. Messages are only sent once a message has been received from neighbours but the target-node in questions (see also Sec. 2). The set $\tilde{V}_e$ is the union of (a) the variables in the subgraph $G'_{\underline{e}}$ with a (remote or direct) neighbour not in $G'_{\underline{e}}$ and (b) the variables not in $G'_{\underline{e}}$ that are in the domain of a factor in $G'_{\underline{e}}$. We denote the variable nodes not contained in V_e with $\overline{V_e} = V \setminus V_e$ and similarly for factor nodes.

$$\begin{aligned} \tilde{V}^a_{\underline{e}} &= \{i \in V_e : \tilde{N}(i) \cap \overline{A_e} \neq \varnothing\} \\ \tilde{V}^b_{\underline{e}} &= \{i \in \overline{V_e} : \tilde{N}(i) \cap A_e \neq \varnothing\} \\ \tilde{V}_e &= \tilde{V}^a_{\underline{e}} \cup \tilde{V}^b_{\underline{e}} \end{aligned} \tag{3.1}$$

For messages in the inverse direction, $\tilde{V}_{\underline{e}\to\overline{e}} = \tilde{V}_{\overline{e}\to\underline{e}}$. This follows directly from (3.1) by replacing the sets V_e and A_e with their complement.

The integer $c_{e,i}$ counts how many nodes related to i (neighbours of i and i itself) are contained in the sending subgraph $G'_{\underline{e}}$. This value is updated locally before

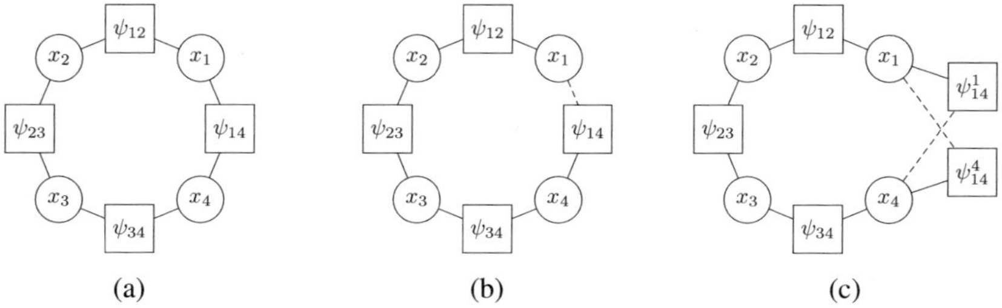

Figure 3.1: The loopy factor graph in (a) transforms into the factor tree-graph with remote neighbours (b) where x_1 and ψ_{14} are their respective remote neighbour. The transformed factor graph in (c) contains a split factor. The transformed graph gives results for variable assignments equivalent to the graph in (a) if $\psi_{14}(x_{14}) = \psi_{14^1}(x_{14}) + \psi_{14^4}(x_{14})$.

sending a message m_e.

$$c_{e,i} = \mathbb{1}_{i \in \tilde{N}(\underline{e})} + \mathbb{1}_{\underline{e}=i} + \sum_{k \in N(\underline{e}) \setminus \{\overline{e}\}} c_{k \rightarrow \underline{e},i} \tag{3.2}$$

Implicitly, $c_{e,i} = 0$ if it is not defined in the message m_e. The indicator function $\mathbb{1}$ evaluates to one if the supplied condition is true and zero otherwise. Note that (3.2) is formulated both for sending variable nodes and sending factor nodes.

Proposition 1 *A variable i is contained in $\tilde{V}_e$ if and only if $0 < c_{e,i} < |\tilde{N}(i)| + 1$.*

PROOF. Since G'_e is a tree-graph and only factors in $\tilde{N}(i)$ and the variable node i itself can add to (3.2), $c_{e,i}$ is bounded with $c_{e,i} \in \{0, \ldots, |\tilde{N}(i)| + 1\}$. Firstly, if $c_{e,i} = 0$, then neither is $i \in V_e$, nor is there a factor α, such that $\alpha \in A_e \cap \tilde{N}(i)$ as any of these conditions would have increased $c_{e,i}$ in (3.2). It follows from (3.1) that $i \notin \tilde{V}_e$. The inverse argument proceeds analogously. Secondly, assume that $i \in \tilde{V}_e$ and $c_{e,i} = |\tilde{N}(i)| + 1$. If $i \in \tilde{V}_e^a$, then $c_{e,i} < |\tilde{N}(i)| + 1$ since at least one neighbour factor $\alpha \in \tilde{N}(i)$ is not contained in A_e and has not contributed to (3.2). If $i \in \tilde{V}_e^b$, then $c_{e,i} < |\tilde{N}(i)| + 1$ with a similar argument. This contradicts the assumption. Lastly, let $c_{e,i}$ such that $0 < c_{e,i} < |\tilde{N}(i)| + 1$. If i is contained in V_e, then $\tilde{N}(i) \cap \overline{A_e}$ is nonempty as $c_{e,i}$ would equal $|\tilde{N}(i)| + 1$ otherwise. If i is not contained in V_e, then $\tilde{N}(i) \cap A_e$ is nonempty as $c_{e,i}$ would equal zero otherwise. It follows from the exhaustion of cases that $i \in \tilde{V}_e \Leftrightarrow 0 < c_{e,i} < |\tilde{N}(i)| + 1$. □

Together with the $c_{e,i}$, the number of i's (direct and remote) neighbours $|\tilde{N}(i)|$ is contained in $\tilde{m}_e$. Thus, extended messages can be constructed with information received via extended messages from neighbour nodes and locally available information. The difference to the original Max-Sum is that the domain $\mathcal{X}_e = \prod_{i \in \tilde{V}_e} \mathcal{X}_i$ of the message function $\bar{m}_e$ may be comprised of multiple variables. Let the *extended domain* of any (factor or variable) node ν be $\mathcal{X}_{\nu^+} = \prod_{i \in \nu^+} \mathcal{X}_i$, $\nu^+ = \{i : \exists k \in N(\nu), i \in \tilde{V}_{k \to \nu}\}$. The value of every $\bar{m}_e(x_e)$ is computed by taking the maximum over all $y \in \mathcal{X}_{\underline{e}^+} : \forall i \in \tilde{V}_e, y_i = (x_e)_i$ by taking the sum of the relevant messages (from all direct neighbours but the target $\overline{e}$) and the local factor $\psi_{\underline{e}}$ on the variable assignment y. If $\underline{e}$ is a variable node, of course $\psi_{\underline{e}}$ evaluates to zero.

$$\bar{m}_e(x_e) = \max_{x_{\underline{e}^+} \setminus \tilde{V}_e} \left[\psi_{\underline{e}}(x_{\underline{e}}) + \sum_{\substack{g=(k \to \underline{e}),\\ k \in N(\underline{e}) \setminus \overline{e}}} \bar{m}_g(x_g) \right] \tag{3.3}$$

Proposition 2 *Let G' be a factor tree-graph with remote neighbours representing a function f. After completing a forwards/backwards schedule, the extended messages exchanged on G' have converged and the max-marginal of the variable $i \in V$ on f can be computed as*

$$f_i^*(x_i) = \max_{\substack{y \in \mathcal{X},\\ y_i = x_i}} f(y) = \max_{x_{i^+} \setminus \{i\}} \sum_{\substack{g=(k \to i),\\ k \in N(i)}} \bar{m}_g(x_g) .$$

PROOF. Messages $\bar{m}_e$ on a tree-graph do not depend on any information from messages sent by the (currently) receiving node $\overline{e}$. Therefore, after the forwards/backwards schedule has completed, every updated message $\bar{m}_e$ according to (3.3) is identical to the message that has last been sent over e.

Next, we show that the value of a message function $\bar{m}_e(x_e)$ for a given x_e equals the summed factor-values in the sending subgraph V_e where all variables in $\tilde{V}_e$ are assigned according to x_e and the variables in V_e without (remote) neighbours outside of G_e are assigned to maximize the sum of factors in G_e.

$$\bar{m}_e(x_e) = \max_{\substack{x \in \mathcal{X}_{V_e \cup \tilde{V}_e},\\ \forall i \in \tilde{V}_e, x_i = (x_e)_i}} \sum_{\alpha \in A_e} \psi_\alpha(x_\alpha)$$

Note that $V_e \cup \tilde{V}_e = \bigcup_{\alpha \in A_e} \tilde{N}(\alpha)$ contains all variables that are the (remote) neighbour of any factor in A_e. Recall that variables i are max-marginalized out during the message construction (3.3) only if $i \in V_e \setminus \tilde{V}_e$, i.e. if no factor outside of G_e is a (remote) neighbour of i. That means the distributive law on the Max-Sum commutative semiring can be applied [AM00]. For example:

$$\max_{x_1,x_2} \left[\psi_1(x_1) + \psi_{12}(x_1, x_2) \right] = \max_{x_1} \left[\psi(x_1) + \max_{x_2} \psi(x_1, x_2) \right]$$

The argument is applied recursively until the leaf nodes are reached, for which it holds trivially.

Now, assume that variable i has received messages $\tilde{m}_{\alpha \to i}$ from all neighbours $\alpha \in N(i)$. For every selected $x_i \in \mathcal{X}_i$ we then have locally available information on the maximum summed factor-values that can be achieved in the subgraphs behind all outgoing edges, i.e. the entire graph. □

Proposition 3 *On a tree-like factor graph G without remote neighbours, the message functions $\bar{m}$ exchanged in Max-Sum with Remote Factors are equal to the corresponding messages m of the original Max-Sum algorithm up to normalization.*

PROOF. For this, we show that the domain of the extended messages exchanged between any factor α and variable i is $\mathcal{X}_i$ and therefore $\tilde{V}_{i \to \alpha} = \tilde{V}_{\alpha \to i} = \{i\}$. If the sending node is the variable node i, then $\tilde{V}^a_{i \to \alpha} = \{i\}$ since no other variable in $V_{i \to \alpha}$ has a neighbour in $\overline{V_{i \to \alpha}}$. Also, $\tilde{V}^b_{i \to \alpha} = \varnothing$ since no variable node in $\overline{V_{i \to \alpha}}$ has a neighbouring factor in $V_{i \to \alpha}$. This follows directly from G being a tree-graph. Similar arguments hold for messages from α to i. Since the domain of the exchanged messages on G is identical, it is easy to see that (2.1) and (3.3) are equivalent when $\kappa = 0$ (normalization is not required for convergence on trees). Since the message functions sent from the leaf nodes do not depend on received messages, they are identical for Max-Sum and Max-Sum with Remote Neighbours and consequently all $\bar{m}_e = m_e$. □

4 Evaluation

This section presents the results of a simple scenario that compares the proposed algorithm in comparison with loopy messsage passing. The algorithm implementation and the scenario example can be accessed online at `https://github.com/jpfr/pygmalion`.

The scenario consists of eight variables, each with a finite, nominal scale of size 5, and eight factors linking the variables to form two connected circles according to Fig. 4.1. The factor functions ψ_α map each element in their domain to a scalar that was randomly sampled from the uniform distribution on $[0, 1]$ during instantiation. The goal is then to find the variable assignment that maximizes the sum of all factors. For Max-Sum with Remote Factors, we removed two edges so that the transformed graph forms a connected tree as can be seen in Fig. 4.1. The size of the scenario is such that brute-force search (in 5^8 possible solutions) can still be applied to verify the results.

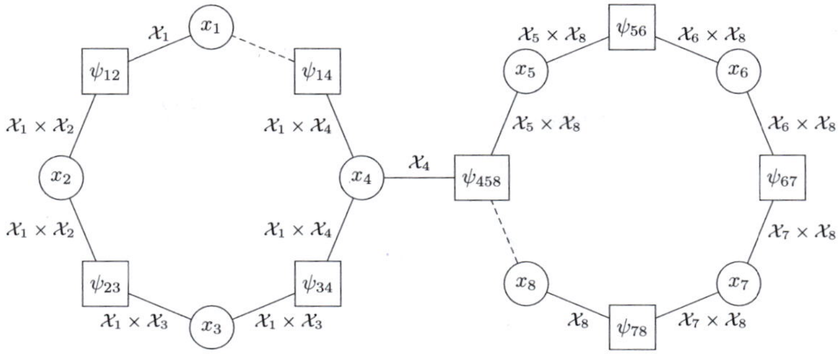

Figure 4.1: The factor graph with remote factors in the example scenario. Dashed edges have been removed for Max-Sum with Remote Factors. The remaining edges are annotated with the domain of the message-functions $\bar{m}_e$ that are passed over it.

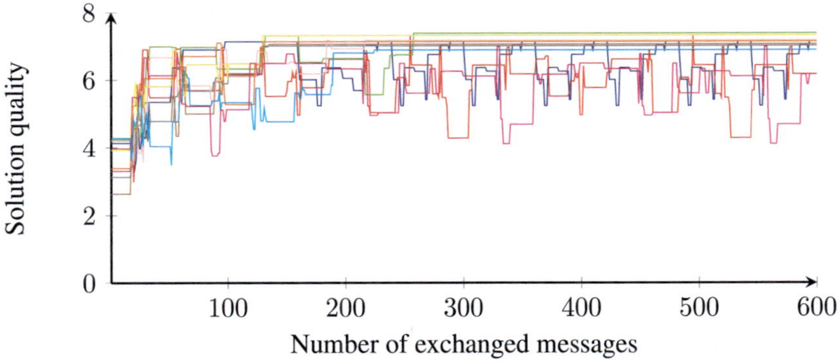

Figure 4.2: Performance of loopy Max-Sum message passing on 10 instances of the scenario. The instances that have not converged after 600 messages show a recurring pattern that is repeated indefinitely.

Figure 4.2 shows the result of Max-Sum on the loopy graph. At every time t all nodes send message to all of their neighbours if these messages are different from the preceding ones. The variable assignments after every message exchange were computed by taking the (running) max-marginal of each variable nodes and maximizing it locally. It can be seen, that inference with Max-Sum can be quite irratic and does not converge in all scenario instances.

By contrast, Max-Sum with Remote Neighbours takes only 30 messages (one forwards/backwards schedule) to infer the maximum solution for all scenario instances. The average message size increase compared to Max-Sum is less than 5, i.e. the domain size of the variables that were made remote neighbours. Figure 4.2 also shows the domain of the message-functions $\bar{m}_e$ passed over the edges. Note how the domain-size increase due to a missing edge is *loop-local* and does not spill over into the adjacent loop. This is an indicator that Max-Sum with Remote Neighbours will perform well for many important applications. Extensive benchmarks and comparison with other DCOP approaches are currently being developed.

5 Conclusion

In this paper, we introduced Max-Sum with Remote Neighbours, a method for the exact inference of maximum utility solutions in distributed constraint optimization settings. This method generalizes the original Max-Sum, that is widely used for DCOP applications, and makes it applicable to settings where the agent communication is constraints and the communication graph does not match the agents utility inter-dependencies. The only requirement for our method is that the communication graph is still connected. The performance of Max-Sum with Remote Neighbours was evaluated on an example scenario. We also applied our method on loopy graphs where some communication links were cut in order to form a tree-graph. Here, it showed superior performance compared to applying the original Max-Sum on loopy graphs, as is often done in practice. It is an open question which links to remove to minimize the inference complexity. Here, we suspect a rich connection to the large body of work dealing with the decomposition of graphs into junction trees with a minimized tree-width.

Bibliography

[AM00] Srinivas M Aji and Robert J McEliece. The generalized distributive law. *Information Theory, IEEE Transactions on*, 46(2):325–343, 2000.

[BM10] Ismel Brito and Pedro Meseguer. Cluster tree elimination for distributed constraint optimization with quality guarantees. *Fundamenta Informaticae*, 102(3):263–286, 2010.

[FRPJ08] Alessandro Farinelli, Alex Rogers, Adrian Petcu, and Nicholas R Jennings. Decentralised coordination of low-power embedded devices using the max-sum algorithm. In *Proceedings of the 7th international joint conference on Autonomous agents and multiagent systems-Volume 2*, pages 639–646, 2008.

[KFL01] Frank R Kschischang, Brendan J Frey, and H-A Loeliger. Factor graphs and the sum-product algorithm. *Information Theory, IEEE Transactions on*, 47(2):498–519, 2001.

[KV06] Jelle R. Kok and Nikos Vlassis. Using the max-plus algorithm for multiagent decision making in coordination graphs. In *Robot Soccer World Cup IX*, pages 1–12. Springer, 2006.

[MSTY05] Pragnesh Jay Modi, Wei-Min Shen, Milind Tambe, and Makoto Yokoo. ADOPT: Asynchronous distributed constraint optimization with quality guarantees. *Artificial Intelligence*, 161(1):149–180, 2005.

[MTB+04] Rajiv T Maheswaran, Milind Tambe, Emma Bowring, Jonathan P Pearce, and Pradeep Varakantham. Taking DCOP to the real world: Efficient complete solutions for distributed multi-event scheduling. In *Proceedings of the Third International Joint Conference on Autonomous Agents and Multiagent Systems*, pages 310–317, 2004.

[PF05] Adrian Petcu and Boi Faltings. DPOP: A Scalable Method for Multiagent Constraint Optimization. In *Proceedings of the International Joint Conferences on Artificial Intelligence (IJCAI)*, pages 266–271, 2005.

[PGCMRA11] Marc Pujol-Gonzalez, Jesus Cerquides, Pedro Meseguer, and Juan A Rodriguez-Aguilar. Communication-constrained DCOPs: Message approximation in GDL with function filtering. In *The 10th International Conference on Autonomous Agents and Multiagent Systems-Volume 1*, pages 379–386. International Foundation for Autonomous Agents and Multiagent Systems, 2011.

[VRAC11] Meritxell Vinyals, Juan A Rodriguez-Aguilar, and Jesús Cerquides. Constructing a unifying theory of dynamic programming DCOP algorithms via the generalized distributive law. *Autonomous Agents and Multi-Agent Systems*, 22(3):439–464, 2011.

[YFW05] Jonathan S Yedidia, William T Freeman, and Yair Weiss. Constructing free-energy approximations and generalized belief propagation algorithms. *Information Theory, IEEE Transactions on*, 51(7):2282–2312, 2005.

Realistic Texture Extraction for 3D Face Models Robust to Self-Occlusion

Chengchao Qu

Vision and Fusion Laboratory
Institute for Anthropomatics and Robotics
Karlsruhe Institute of Technology (KIT), Germany
qu@kit.edu

Technical Report IES-2014-08

Abstract: In the context of face modeling, probably the most well-known approach to represent 3D faces is the 3D Morphable Model (3DMM). When 3DMM is fitted to a 2D image, the shape as well as the texture and illumination parameters are simultaneously estimated. However, if real facial texture is needed, texture extraction from the 2D image is necessary. This paper addresses the problems in texture extraction of a single image caused by self-occlusion. Unlike common approaches that leverage the symmetric property of the face by mirroring the visible facial part, which is sensitive to inhomogeneous illumination, this work first generates a virtual texture map for the skin area iteratively by averaging the color of neighbored vertices. Although this step creates unrealistic, overly smoothed texture, illumination stays constant between the real and virtual texture. In the second pass, the mirrored texture is gradually blended with the real or generated texture according to the visibility. This scheme ensures a gentle handling of illumination and yet yields realistic texture. Because the blending area only relates to non-informative area, main facial features still have unique appearance in different face halves. Evaluation results reveal realistic rendering in novel poses robust to challenging illumination conditions and small registration errors.

1 Introduction

Facial analysis has attracted increasing attention in the computer vision and pattern recognition community despite decades of research and application. 3D face modeling has been widely used and proven to be effective in face recognition [BV03] and animation [BBPV03]. Probably the most well-known approach to represent 3D faces is the 3D Morphable Model (3DMM) proposed by Blanz and Vetter

[BV99]. Separate linear subspaces for shape and texture are learned by Principal Component Analysis (PCA) for a compact representation of the respective variations. When 3DMM is fitted to a 2D image, not only the shape coefficients, but also the texture and illumination parameters are simultaneously estimated, resulting in a huge parameter space.

The complete 3DMM fitting takes account of the learned PCA texture model and Phong illumination to minimize the fitting error of shape and appearance. To address the efficiency problem, a series of optimization efforts are made to allow for faster convergence [RV03] and larger convexity basin to avoid local minima [RV05] by introducing more image features (*e.g.*, specular highlight and edge constraint) than just pixel intensity. These methods can reconstruct the texture parameters including the occluded facial part according to the 3DMM dataset and the estimated illumination at the cost of computational time, making these algorithms inappropriate for online applications. From another perspective, when artificially rendered texture is not desired, *e.g.*, for forensic analysis, facial texture extraction from the 2D image is necessary.

As an alternative that is tailored to the above requirements, dependency on the facial appearance in the fitting can be completely abandoned and the 3D shape can be inferred solely based on a few dozens of sparse 2D feature points, allowing for real-time reconstruction. In the approach of Blanz *et al.* [BMVS04], using several manually annotated 2D feature points, the complete 3D shape and camera projection are reconstructed in closed-form by least squares fitting. Prior knowledge from the 3DMM dataset is utilized to solve this otherwise ill-posed problem. Since the texture is yet to be extracted from the image afterwards, the color values of the image are mapped to the vertices on the 3D model. However, the complex geometry of human faces results in self-occluded facial regions even for a frontal pose.

To alleviate the self-occlusion problem after texture extraction, a posterior step to estimate the global 3DMM texture parameters by assuming photometric invariance [AS10] is still applicable. For real texture extraction, Blanz *et al.* [BMVS04] reflect the visible part to fill the missing color values. At places where both parts are occluded, the average texture of 3DMM is applied. The strict constraints of constant skin and illumination can impose severe artifacts on the occluded textured face model. Similarly, the $3/4$ profile face ($\pm 45°$) is regarded as the most representative pose for texture extraction by Roy-Chowdhury *et al.* [RCCG05] and the mirroring approach is employed for occlusion handling. On the other hand, Jiang *et al.* [JHY$^+$05] interpolate the blank area by averaging the intensity of the connected vertices. Because the algorithm only accepts frontal faces, the smearing effect introduced by interpolation only appears near the neck and ears, which is not crucial to the overall visual quality. Combining multiple images from different viewpoints yields more realistic results than interpolation [PHL+98]. Although the seamless blending constraint is carefully designed to handle inhomogeneous illumination, only results of studio face images in controlled environment are shown [PHL+98, ZCS06].

This paper addresses the possible problems in texture extraction and proposes a straightforward solution to generate realistic facial texture for self-occluded regions. This approach assumes the 3D shape of the face is already recovered. After registering the shape back to the 2D image, small displacements caused by the limited 3DMM subspace are dealt with by triangulation and warping. To overcome the self-occlusion problem, unlike the above mentioned approaches in the literature, which either is sensitive to illumination or generates interpolation artifacts, in this work, we combine the advantages of both approaches. The "bad" half of the face is first determined. Starting from the cheek near the nose area, a virtual texture map for the homogeneous area is created iteratively by averaging the color of neighboring visible vertices until the whole face is filled artificially. Although this step creates unrealistic, overly smoothed texture, illumination stays constant between the real and virtual texture. In the second pass, the mirrored texture is gradually blended with increasing weight. At places where the original vertices are visible, the real texture is used, otherwise, the generated texture is taken for blending. This scheme ensures a gentle handling of illumination and yet yields realistic texture. Because the blending area only relates to non-informative area, main facial features, *i.e.*, eyes and mouth, still have unique appearance in different face halves, which is proven to be crucial to face recognition [LSCM03]. The effectiveness of our approach is evaluated on several "in the wild" images and videos containing diverse pose and illumination variations.

The remainder of this paper is organized as follows. A brief introduction to 3DMM and efficient fitting using 2D feature landmarks is given in §2 and §3 respectively. The procedure of the proposed facial texture extraction framework is discussed in detail in §4. The qualitative results are demonstrated in §5. Finally, we conclude our work in §6.

2 3D Morphable Model

The 3D Morphable Model, introduced by Blanz and Vetter [BV99], is a class-specific model to describe 3D objects, especially human faces. 3DMM is composed of 3D geometry and texture constructed from 3D laser scans of human heads. After preprocessing to fill the holes from laser scans, the dense set with a fixed size of p vertices is put into full point-to-point correspondence by optical flow, so that morphing between faces is possible. As an example, the first shape and texture entry corresponds to the tip of the nose across all 3D faces in Fig. 2.1(a). The shape is represented in a vectorized form $\mathbf{s} = \{x_1, y_1, z_1, x_2, y_2, z_2, \ldots, x_p, y_p, z_p\} \in \mathbb{R}^{3p}$. Different from its sibling Active Appearance Model (AAM) [CET98], where the texture is defined as the 2D image inside the convex hull of the feature points, the 3D texture is modeled on each of the p vertices as $\mathbf{t} = \{r_1, g_1, b_1, r_2, g_2, b_2, \ldots, r_p, g_p, b_p\} \in \mathbb{R}^{3p}$. By applying PCA on all face scans, the shape and texture can be expressed as a convex combination of mean vectors $\bar{\mathbf{s}}$ and $\bar{\mathbf{t}}$ and the eigenvectors

$$\mathbf{s} = \bar{\mathbf{s}} + \mathbf{S}\,\mathrm{diag}(\boldsymbol{\sigma})\boldsymbol{\alpha}, \quad \mathbf{t} = \bar{\mathbf{t}} + \mathbf{T}\,\mathrm{diag}(\boldsymbol{\tau})\boldsymbol{\beta}.$$

The columns of matrices $\mathbf{S} \in \mathbb{R}^{3p\times m}$ and $\mathbf{T} \in \mathbb{R}^{3p\times m}$ are m eigenvectors and $\boldsymbol{\sigma} \in \mathbb{R}^m$ and $\boldsymbol{\tau} \in \mathbb{R}^m$ are the eigenvalues of the shape and texture respectively. Thus, given the registered 3D scans, 3DMM is mathematically represented as the set $\{\bar{\mathbf{s}}, \mathbf{S}, \boldsymbol{\sigma}, \bar{\mathbf{t}}, \mathbf{T}, \boldsymbol{\tau}\}$ and a novel face can be described using the 3DMM coefficients $\{\boldsymbol{\alpha}, \boldsymbol{\beta}\}$ inside the spanned subspace of the training data.

Due to the heavy workload for acquiring, processing and annotating 3D data, there are few public 3DMM datasets available. In this work, we utilize the Basel Face Model (BFM) from Paysan *et al.* within the group of Prof. Vetter [PKA+09], who is the originator of 3DMM [BV99]. In BFM, besides the usual trained 3DMM parameters $\{\bar{\mathbf{s}}, \mathbf{S}, \boldsymbol{\sigma}, \bar{\mathbf{t}}, \mathbf{T}, \boldsymbol{\tau}\}$, a manually annotated mask to separate the area of the two eyes, the nose, the mouth and the rest skin region is also included, which is highlighted in Fig. 2.1(b). We make full use of this segmentation mask in our texture extraction method in §4.

3 3D Shape Reconstruction

3D shape reconstruction based on only a few 2D feature points offers a computationally efficient alternative compared to the complete 3DMM fitting with regard to the albedo, illumination and other image features. Blanz *et al.* [BMVS04] propose a non-iterative solution to recover the non-rigid shape deformation and the rigid motion simultaneously. For a set of $f \ll p$ sparse facial landmarks, the 2D coordinates on the image plane $\mathbf{y} \in \mathbb{R}^{2f}$ can be expressed as a linear combination of the projected 3D shape variations of the 3DMM. Assuming that the measurements are subject to uncorrelated Gaussian noise, the error function of 2D and 3D projection is equivalent to

$$\epsilon = ||\mathbf{Qc} - \mathbf{y}||^2 + \eta||\mathbf{c}||^2$$

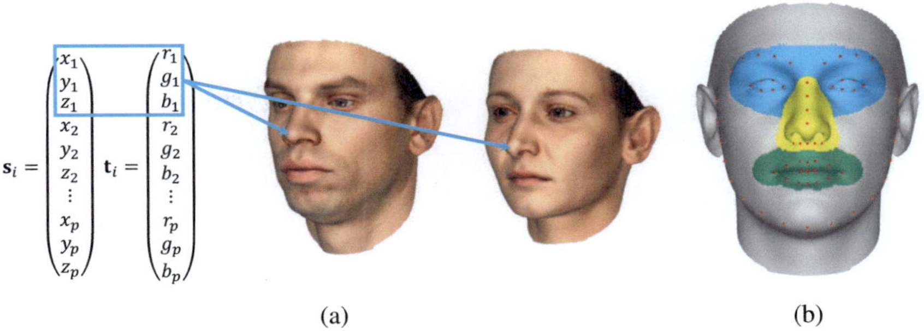

Figure 2.1: (a) The same shape and texture entries correspond to the same vertex on the face mesh (*e.g.*, tip of the nose in the example) (b) Mask with the four segments (*i.e.*, eyes, nose, mouth and the rest) and the manually annotated 66 feature landmarks on the BFM dataset

in Bayesian Maximum a Posteriori (MAP) formulation, where $\mathbf{Q}$ combines the PCA eigenvectors of 3DMM, the known 3D-2D mapping and the projection, while $\mathbf{c}$ contains the 3DMM shape coefficients $\boldsymbol{\alpha}$. Blanz *et al.* [BMVS04] linearize the rotation, scaling and translation in the form of extra eigenvectors and shape coefficients, which are attached to $\mathbf{Q}$ and $\mathbf{c}$ respectively. In this way, a straightforward closed-form solution

$$\mathbf{c} = (\mathbf{Q}^\top \mathbf{Q} + \eta \mathbf{I})^\dagger \mathbf{Q}^\top \mathbf{y}$$

in ridge regression is made possible and an initial pose estimation is not necessary.

The 2D sparse feature points are either manually annotated or localized by face alignment methods. Faggian *et al.* [FPS06] first integrate a generative person-specific AAM to localize the 2D coordinates of the feature landmarks to reconstruct the 3D dense face shape automatically. We build on our previous work [QMSB14], where the inconsistent 2D AAM and 3DMM landmark position emerging in the self-occluded area is addressed and 3D face reconstruction robust to pose changes for both static images and videos is proposed. The 66-point AAM landmarks are mapped to the BFM mesh as the prior 3D-2D correspondence for the automatic process. Fig. 2.1(b) illustrates the feature point scheme used in this paper. The reader is referred to [BMVS04, QMSB14] for details.

(a) (b) (c)

Figure 4.1: (a) An example input image (b) 2D landmarks (c) Projection of the 3D landmarks from the reconstructed 3D dense shape on the warped image

4 Texture Extraction

After 3D shape reconstruction in §3, the 3DMM shape coefficients $\boldsymbol{\alpha}$ as well as the pose are recovered. Since the texture parameters $\boldsymbol{\beta}$ are not available compared to complete 3DMM fitting, we extract the texture from the image directly. All interim stages for generating realistic texture under non-frontal poses are detailed in this section. As a graphical example, the George Clooney image downloaded from the Internet[1] in Fig. 4.1(a) is reconstructed step by step.

4.1 Extraction of Visible Texture

Existing 3D face reconstruction methods mostly focus on the quality of reconstructed shape and do not elaborate on the texture extraction stage, which is only roughly mentioned within a few words, *e.g.*, "the color values of the image are mapped as a texture on the surface" [BMVS04] or "the 2D image is directly mapped to the 3D geometry" [JHY$^+$05]. However, we find that it is nontrivial to generate realistic texture for 3D models. To start from scratch, there are several problems to be solved. The first one is the limitation of the linear 3DMM subspace.

A 3DMM is usually trained with a few hundred 3D face scans, *e.g.*, 100 for the original work [BV99], 200 for BFM [PKA$^+$09], hence, the spanned PCA subspace has only a limited power to describe novel faces. As a result, the reconstructed 3D shape cannot always fit the 2D image perfectly. The deviation can be measured at the aligned 2D landmarks and the projected 3D correspondence. In Figs. 4.1(b)

[1] `http://img.timeinc.net/time/photoessays/2007/george_clooney/george_clooney_01.jpg`

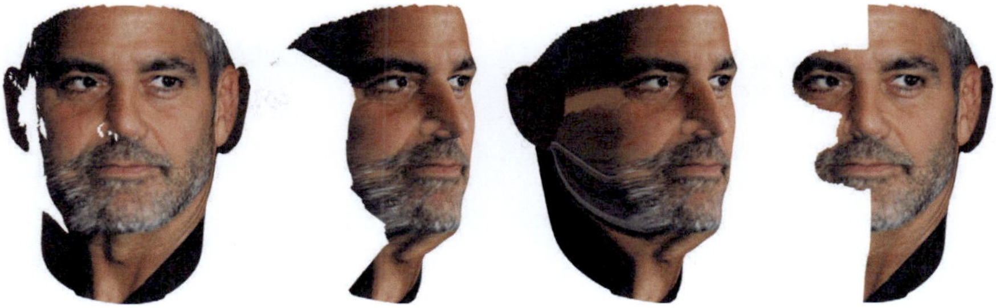

(a) (b) (c) (d)

Figure 4.2: Steps of texture extraction and generation: (a) Visible texture after extraction (b) Texture after erasing vertices near the visible boundary (c) Filled texture with interpolation (d) Initial texture for iterative blending

and 4.1(c), the lower points of the nose and the left face contour are slightly different. To compensate the small offset, auxiliary points are added around the face to perform Delaunay triangulation and subsequently piecewise warping. Thanks to the dense 3D registration for shape and pose, only little correction is needed, hence, we are free of the unnatural visual affect by warping sparse AAM meshes [GES09]. The result is demonstrated in Fig. 4.1(c).

On account of the large number of vertices, it is common that multiple vertices are projected to the same image pixel. Visibility detection thus determines to which vertex or vertices the color value of the certain image pixel should be assigned. One choice is to use the z-buffer algorithm [PHL$^+$98]. After rendering the 3D shape with the recovered pose parameters, the depth map of the scene is generated by comparing the depth of each vertex. Only the ones closest to the camera are set to visible. Alternatively, we utilize a simple and efficient hidden point detection algorithm by Katz *et al.* [KTB07]. Occlusion is determined with the vertices alone without the knowledge of surface and normal, *etc.* Afterwards, the color values on the visible vertices are extracted with non-uniform interpolation. The result in Fig. 4.2(a) shows few errors and outliers.

4.2 Inference of Occluded Texture

Existing research is already aware of the self-occlusion problem of the AAM landmarks for 3D shape reconstruction [QMSB14, LLP$^+$12]. However, to the best of our knowledge, no prior work is dedicated to generating natural texture for the hidden facial area. To make better understanding of our approach, we first introduce a few useful operations. In order to infer the missing texture iteratively, we need to find out the invisible vertices that are adjacent to the visible ones. Formally, given a set of visible and occluded vertices $\{\mathbf{V}, \overline{\mathbf{V}}\}$ and a set of edges $\mathbf{E}$ in the 3D mesh, these candidates are defined as

$$\mathbf{V}_{\oplus} = \{v | v \in \overline{\mathbf{V}} \wedge \exists v' \in \mathbf{V} : (v, v') \in \mathbf{E}\}. \tag{4.1}$$

On the contrary, the set of vertices to be removed are denoted as

$$\mathbf{V}_{\ominus} = \{v | v \in \mathbf{V} \wedge \exists v' \in \overline{\mathbf{V}} : (v, v') \in \mathbf{E}\}. \tag{4.2}$$

To interpolate a hidden vertex $v \in \overline{\mathbf{V}}$, its color value $g(v)$ is the average color of the adjacent visible vertices

$$g(v) = \frac{\sum_{v' \in \mathbf{\Omega}} g(v')}{|\mathbf{\Omega}|}, \text{ where } \mathbf{\Omega} = \{v' | v' \in \mathbf{V} \wedge (v, v') \in \mathbf{E}\}. \tag{4.3}$$

Back to Fig. 4.2(a), the boundary texture near the occluded region shows some smearing effect. Comparison with the localized 2D landmarks in Fig. 4.1(b) suggest that the landmark noise and the nearly perpendicular normal direction in this area make the mapped texture prone to quality degradation. Therefore, the boundary region of the "bad" half of face is eliminated by a sequence of removal operations applied to the vertex set $\mathbf{V}_{\ominus}$ in Eq. (4.2). Note that we preserve the facial features, *i.e.*, eyes, nose and mouth, by applying the BFM segmentation mask (see Fig. 2.1(b)) and only clear the skin texture, yielding Fig. 4.2(b).

Some approaches leverage the symmetric property of the face by just mirroring the visible part of the face and provide some good-looking results on well illuminated images [BMVS04, RCCG05]. Obviously, the example image Fig. 4.3(c) highlights two drawbacks of this simple strategy. First, even minor illumination difference between the mirrored parts will result in severe inhomogeneous intensity and poor visual effect. On the other hand, some facial regions, *e.g.*, between the chin and neck, are often invisible in both face halves. To deal with these problems, a virtual texture map is first generated by filling the missing color values by iteratively interpolating $\mathbf{V}_{\oplus}$ according to Eqs. (4.1) and (4.3). As can be seen in Fig. 4.2(c), although the filled texture is overly smoothed and lacks high-frequency details, the illumination remains constant.

In the final stage, this virtual texture map is blended with the mirrored visible half of face. The basic principle of blending is to maximize the usage of the "good" half of the face while keeping the unique features, *e.g.*, the left and right eye, distinguishable. For this purpose, again the BFM segmentation mask (see Fig. 2.1(b)) offers an effective way to preserve only the best and most important facial texture. An example texture before the fusion process is given in Fig. 4.2(d). Starting

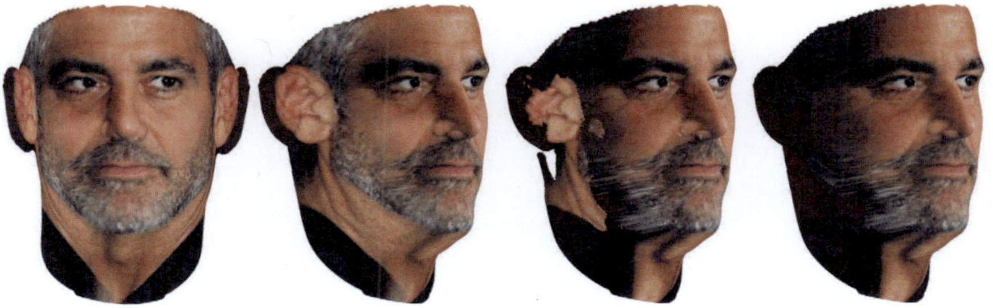

(a) (b) (c) (d)

Figure 4.3: Final result of the proposed method for Fig. 4.1(a) in (a) frontal view and (b) novel view compared to (c) texture mirroring and (d) interpolation

from this initial map, texture of new vertices selected by Eq. (4.1) are fused in an iterative manner with increasing weight

$$g(v) = \lambda(i)g_{\text{mirror}}(v) + (1 - \lambda(i))g_{\text{interpolation}}(v), \text{ where } \lambda(i) = \min\{\frac{i}{N}, 1\}.$$

$i \in \mathbb{N}$ denotes the iteration counter and N is the length of the blending process. The final result in Figs. 4.3(a) and 4.3(b) demonstrates that both smooth illumination transition and texture details even the beard are well preserved. The simple mirroring approach in Fig. 4.3(c) lacks a texture region under the ear, which is also invisible in the original face half. Moreover, abrupt texture transition and artifacts caused by registration error further degrade the visual quality. Fig. 4.3(d) looks overly smoothed and shows smearing artifact. A boundary of different intensity can be seen, indicating the opposite paths of the iterative interpolation process from the dark region in ear and the middle.

5 Experiments

In this section, the proposed texture extraction approach is compared with the baseline methods on the static Labeled Face Parts in the Wild (LFPW) image dataset [BJKK11] and the YouTube Celebrities video dataset [KKPR08].

LFPW is a relatively new face image dataset for testing face alignment algorithms with annotated landmarks. The images are downloaded from the Internet and contain large variations in pose, illumination, *etc*. As our example in the previous sections, BFM is utilized as our 3DMM for reconstruction. Because of the lack of diverse expressions when capturing BFM, only images that have approximately

Table 5.1: Comparison of the proposed work against baseline methods with regard to illumination consistency and details of the extracted texture

	Mirroring	Interpolation	Proposed work
Illumination consistency	−	+	+
Texture details	+	−	+

neutral expressions are chosen in this experiment. In Fig. 5.1, the frontal view and a novel view of the 3D faces show very realistic texture. Even the originally occluded region is very naturally "hallucinated". Especially, the skin texture of second image is of high resolution, which is transferred and blended from the visible area. No sign of transition between the authentic and the mirrored texture is visible. Furthermore, the shadow on the face contour is neatly neutralized. Similarly, the challenging light casted on the right face half in the third image is well taken care of, too. Contrarily, the mirroring approach is very sensible to the lighting difference between the two face halves. A hard boundary line is seen in most examples. For the interpolation-based method, only overly smoothed texture without any useful details is generated, which is only applicable to fill small blank areas [JHY+05]. Last but not least, the dark or color stripes near the face contour are erroneously extracted from the background, which is inevitable for vertices of nearly perpendicular normal direction in the case of minimal landmark localization error. Our approach that first removes this region before generating virtual texture (see Fig. 4.2(b)) is proven to be quite effective.

Another qualitative evaluation on the YouTube Celebrities video dataset [KKPR08] is performed and the results are illustrated in Fig. 5.2. The dataset is composed of short interviews and TV shows of celebrities and contains low-resolution faces and typical video artifacts. Nevertheless, the well-known facial characteristics of these celebrities are still clearly recognizable in the person-specific 3D models. We summarize the advantages of the proposed approach over the baseline methods in Tab. 5.1.

6 Conclusions

The problem of single image real texture mapping for 3D face models is addressed in this paper. A general extraction workflow for visible texture is first introduced. As the main contribution of this work, a novel iterative blending scheme to draw the advantages of the conventional mirroring and interpolation methods for the occluded face area is proposed, which generates detailed and realistic facial texture

Figure 5.1: Experimental results of the proposed method in frontal (2nd row) and novel view (3rd row) compared to texture mirroring (4th row) and interpolation (5th row) on the LFPW dataset [BJKK11]

Figure 5.2: Experimental results of the proposed method in frontal (2nd row) and novel view (3rd row) on the YouTube Celebrities dataset [KKPR08]

with smooth illumination transition. The effectiveness of the framework is justified on the publicly available "in the wild" images and video data in challenging uncontrolled pose and illumination conditions. An extended algorithm to fuse images of multiple views with careful registration and constraints [PHL$^+$98] can be done as future work.

Bibliography

[AS10] O. Aldrian and W. Smith. A linear approach of 3D face shape and texture recovery using a 3D morphable model. In *BMVC*, pages 75.1–75.10, 2010.

[BBPV03] V. Blanz, C. Basso, T. Poggio, and T. Vetter. Reanimating faces in images and video. *Comput. Gr. Forum*, 22(3):641–650, 2003.

[BJKK11] P. N. Belhumeur, D. W. Jacobs, D. Kriegman, and N. Kumar. Localizing parts of faces using a consensus of exemplars. In *CVPR*, pages 545–552, 2011.

[BMVS04] V. Blanz, A. Mehl, T. Vetter, and H.-P Seidel. A statistical method for robust 3D surface reconstruction from sparse data. In *3DPVT*, pages 293–300, 2004.

[BV99] V. Blanz and T. Vetter. A morphable model for the synthesis of 3D faces. In *SIGGRAPH*, pages 187–194, 1999.

[BV03] V. Blanz and T. Vetter. Face recognition based on fitting a 3D morphable model. *IEEE Trans. Pattern Anal. Mach. Intell.*, 25(9):1063–1074, 2003.

[CET98] T. F. Cootes, G. J. Edwards, and C. J. Taylor. Active appearance models. In *ECCV*, volume 1407, pages 484–498, 1998.

[FPS06] N. Faggian, A. P. Paplinski, and J. Sherrah. Active appearance models for automatic fitting of 3D morphable models. In *AVSS*, page 90, 2006.

[GES09] H. Gao, H. K. Ekenel, and R. Stiefelhagen. Pose normalization for local appearance-based face recognition. In *ICB*, pages 32–41, 2009.

[JHY+05] D. Jiang, Y. Hu, S. Yan, L. Zhang, H. Zhang, and W. Gao. Efficient 3D reconstruction for face recognition. *Pattern Recognition*, 38(6):787–798, 2005.

[KKPR08] M. Kim, S. Kumar, V. Pavlovic, and H. Rowley. Face tracking and recognition with visual constraints in real-world videos. In *CVPR*, pages 1–8, 2008.

[KTB07] S. Katz, A. Tal, and R. Basri. Direct visibility of point sets. In *SIGGRAPH*, page 24, 2007.

[LLP+12] Y. J. Lee, S. J. Lee, K. R. Park, J. Jo, and J. Kim. Single view-based 3D face reconstruction robust to self-occlusion. *EURASIP J. Adv. Signal. Proces.*, 2012(1):176, 2012.

[LSCM03] Yanxi Liu, Karen L. Schmidt, Jeffrey F. Cohn, and Sinjini Mitra. Facial asymmetry quantification for expression invariant human identification. *CVIU*, 91(1–2):138–159, 2003. Special Issue on Face Recognition.

[PHL+98] F. Pighin, J. Hecker, D. Lischinski, R. Szeliski, and D. H. Salesin. Synthesizing realistic facial expressions from photographs. In *SIGGRAPH*, pages 75–84, 1998.

[PKA+09] P. Paysan, R. Knothe, B. Amberg, S. Romdhani, and T. Vetter. A 3D face model for pose and illumination invariant face recognition. In *AVSS*, pages 296–301, 2009.

[QMSB14] C. Qu, E. Monari, T. Schuchert, and J. Beyerer. Fast, robust and automatic 3D face model reconstruction from videos. In *AVSS*, pages 113–118, 2014.

[RCCG05] A. K. Roy-Chowdhury, R. Chellappa, and H. Gupta. 3D face modeling from monocular video sequences. In Rama Chellappa and Wenyi Zhao, editors, *Face Processing: Advanced Modeling and Methods*, chapter 6, pages 185–218, III. Academic Press, 2005.

[RV03] S. Romdhani and T. Vetter. Efficient, robust and accurate fitting of a 3D morphable model. In *CVPR*, pages 59–66, 2003.

[RV05] S. Romdhani and T. Vetter. Estimating 3D shape and texture using pixel intensity, edges, specular highlights, texture constraints and a prior. In *CVPR*, volume 2, pages 986–993, 2005.

[ZCS06] M. Zhao, T.-S. Chua, and T. Sim. Morphable face reconstruction with multiple images. In *FGR*, pages 597–602, 2006.

Methods of learning discriminative features for automated visual inspection

Matthias Richter

Vision and Fusion Laboratory
Institute for Anthropomatics
Karlsruhe Institute of Technology (KIT), Germany
matthias.richter@kit.edu

Technical Report IES-2014-09

Abstract: At the present day, automation of visual inspection tasks is a typical engineering problem. Experts design the physical aspects of the system and devise classification algorithms based on a small sample of the material to be inspected. Much of this work is devoted to finding suitable features to discriminate wanted from unwanted material. In this report, we explore methods to automatically *learn* object descriptors from a suitably large sample. We focus on two types of descriptors: (a) global descriptors, which represent the object as a whole and (b) local descriptors, which focus on topical features. Apart from freeing the engineers to attend to other tasks, these methods allow non-experts to operate and reuse visual inspection systems, e.g. to inspect a different product than originally intended.

1 Introduction

Automated visual inspection is becoming more and more prevalent in many industries, from detection of precious ores and minerals in mining to quality inspection of food. Novel, improved sensors make even more application areas accessible, and the increasing speed of visual inspection systems allows previously unseen throughputs. That development as well as decreasing costs of the hardware components raises the demand even further.

One might think that it would be possible to acquire complete off-the-shelve solutions. While that is true to some degree, adapting existing systems to specific products still remains a complicated endeavour. In many cases there are best practices to approach the design of the physical aspects of the machine (i.e. material transport, lighting and image acquisition, etc.) that require moderate effort to adapt to a given problem. The major engineering bottleneck resides in establishing the classification stage. An expert identifies discriminative features by analyzing a relatively small sample of wanted and unwanted material and then devises algorithms to extract these features from an image. This lengthy process is typically driven by trial-and-error and requires extensive experience on part of the expert.

There are approaches to "widen" this bottleneck by utilizing machine learning techniques. Here, low level-features such as hue-histograms, Gabor filter responses and Fourier shape descriptors are extracted from the images and fed into generic classification algorithms like support vector machines, random forests and artificial neural networks. For encompassing reviews of these methods, see the works of Malamas et al. [MPZ$^+$03], who investigate these approaches in visual inspection in general, and Du and Sun [DS06], who focus their attention to the application to food in particular.

However, these methods are rarely applied in practice. The main reasons are that they require far too much time to compute the features and that the black box nature of the machine learning algorithms prevents users to understand how the visual inspection system derives a decision [BCGS$^+$09].

Additionally, we argue that such an approach misses the original question: What features are characteristic of the material and relevant to the visual inspection problem? In this report, we try to answer this question by answering another: How can one learn discriminative feature transformations from a suitably large sample of wanted and unwanted material?

1.1 Related Work

There seem to be surprisingly few researchers also concerned with this topic. In an early work, Duffy et al. propose to detect burn marks on filters by recording color histograms of images containing defects and images that show intact filters [DCL00]. These histograms are fused into a "true target' histogram that characterizes the burn marks. Defects are then detected by back-projection and thresholding the resulting image. In a follow-up study, Bergasa, Duffy et al. use the same approach, but model only non-defective color using a Gaussian mixture model of the joint red and green color distribution [BDLM00].

Zhang et al. use a similar method to grade date maturity [ZLTL14]. In training, they collect the RG-color histograms of date samples of different maturity grades and compute a back-projection table that maps RG-tuples to a ripeness level. In this table, missing values are filled in by linear interpolation between the neighboring entries, so that every possible color is represented. In testing, fruits are graded by determining the mean gray value in the back-projected image.

Similarly, Li et al. grade the ripeness of tomato fruits by determining dominant colors in images of fruits of different maturity grades [LCG09]. Their method is relatively involved and requires multiple color space conversions and a specialized clustering algorithm. Finally, they define several ripeness classes and compute characteristic histograms of dominant colors in these classes. Unseen tomatoes are classified by comparing the histogram of dominant colors to the ones learned in the training phase.

While all these approaches are concerned with a particular application in mind, Richter and Beyerer propose a method suitable for a wider range of products [RB14]. Similar to Duffy et al. they collect color histograms of the material under inspection and compute a mapping to a semantic attribute in a four step process. Unlike the other approaches, their approach requires a separate classifier that uses the attribute-images to classify objects.

All these methods focus on color as sorting criterion. Therefore, defects that are characterized by a change of texture or shape are undetectable. In the next section, we propose two methods that are able to capture all aspects of object appearance: color, texture and shape.

2 Methods

Feature descriptors can be divided into two groups: global descriptors and local descriptors. The former summarize the object appearance: "The apple is green with a few brown spots". The latter focus on topical features: "There is a small round brown spot near the stem of the apple". Both types of descriptors are applicable in different scenarios. Judging the overall appearance of an object calls for usage of global descriptors, e.g. when grading the surface of tiles or when assessing the ripeness of a fruit. Local descriptors, on the other hand, are applicable when searching for localized defects, for example detection of fungal infection on grains or localization of scratches on surfaces.

In this section, we present approaches to learn either type of descriptor. The first method is based on the bag of visual words (BOV) framework, while the latter utilizes cascades of random ferns.

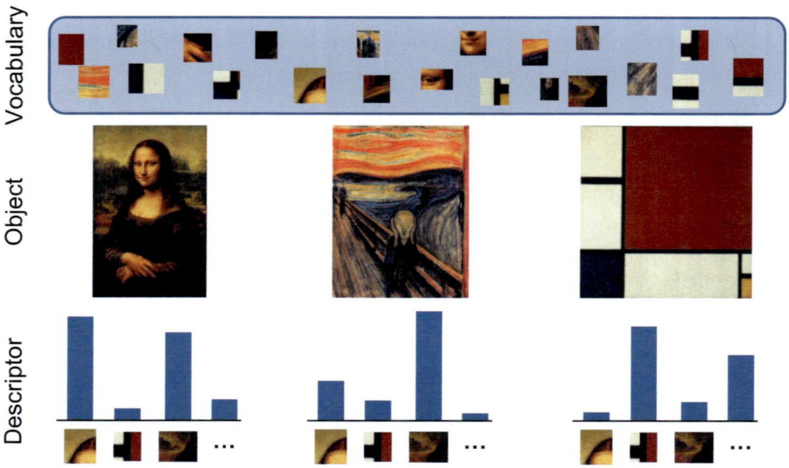

Figure 2.1: Outline of the BOV method: Given a vocabulary of visual words, objects (images) can be characterized by a statistic of the visual words appearing in the image. Note that spatial information is not considered.

2.1 Global Descriptors

Originally introduced by Csurka et al. in the context of image categorization [CDF$^+$04], the bag of visual words model has been applied in many domains such as content based retrieval, face recognition and action classification. The descriptors have many advantages: they are compact, invariant to object scale and rotation and are highly discriminative.

The main idea is to consider images to be documents that are composed of *visual words*. As with text documents, some of the words carry more information than others, that is some words are characteristic of certain objects or concepts, while others may be found in many different images. The task of image categorization can then be approached by constructing a dictionary of discriminative keywords and describing images by determining which words appear in them. This idea is outlined in Figure 2.1. It is formalized in the following.

2.1.1 Vocabulary

Starting from a collection of input images $\mathcal{I}_i$, $i = 1, \ldots, N$, a large set of local low level, D-dimensional feature descriptors $\mathbf{x}_{ti}$, $t = 1, \ldots, T_i$ (e.g. SIFT) are extracted from each image. Here, T_i denotes the number of features extracted from

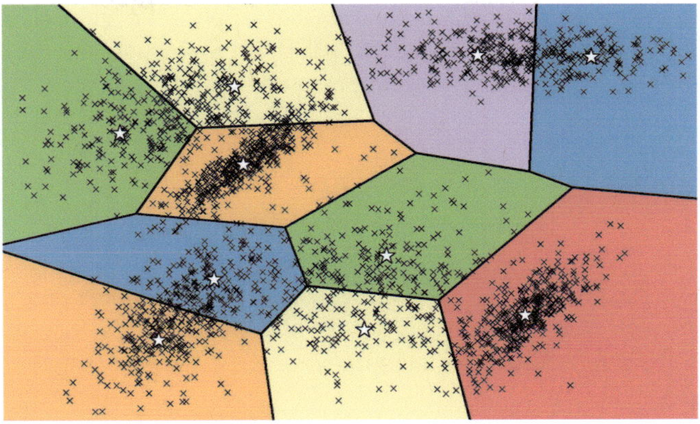

Figure 2.2: Example of hard assignment in two dimensions. Each feature (crosses) is related to the closest of the ten visual words (stars).

$\mathcal{I}_i$ and may vary from image to image. Each $\mathbf{x}_{ti}$ can be interpreted as an "inflection" of a visual word. Visual words correspond to clusters in the feature space. Therefore, keywords can be determined using cluster-analysis. Although other approaches are conceivable, most BOV implementations use a simple K-means clustering or Gaussian mixture models (GMM) with a fixed number of clusters. Csurka et al. noted that the exact number of visual words does have a negligible impact on the classification performance [CDF$^+$04]. A common approach is to repeat the cluster analysis with varying K and keep the clustering that best fits the data.

2.1.2 Descriptors

Now that the vocabulary is determined, the descriptor $\mathbf{m}$ for an image $\mathcal{I}$ is chosen to represent some statistic over the visual words that appear in $\mathcal{I}$. Csurka et al. proposed hard assignment [CDF$^+$04]: The D-dimensional low level features $\mathbf{x}_t$, extracted from $\mathcal{I}$, are assigned to the nearest cluster center (see Fig. 2.2). Each entry m_k in the descriptor $\mathbf{m}$ represents the fraction of features falling into the Voronoi-region around the cluster center $\boldsymbol{\mu}_k$,

$$m_k = \frac{1}{T}\left|\left\{\mathbf{x}_t \middle| \arg\min_{\boldsymbol{\mu}} \|\mathbf{x}_t - \boldsymbol{\mu}\| = \boldsymbol{\mu}_k\right\}\right|.$$

The resulting K-dimensional descriptor represents a simple count statistic of visual words, but does not provide any further information over the "inflection" of the words, i.e. the location of the features in relation to the cluster center. Fisher vectors, introduced by Perronnin et al. [PD07], provide an alternative encoding that enriches the descriptor by first-order statistics of the feature distribution.

The key idea is to assume that the $\mathbf{x}_{ti}$ are generated by a Gaussian mixture,

$$p(\mathbf{x}|\boldsymbol{\lambda}) = \sum_{k=1}^{K} \omega_k g(\mathbf{x}|\boldsymbol{\mu}_k, \Sigma_k),$$

where $\boldsymbol{\lambda} = (\omega_k, \boldsymbol{\mu}_k, \Sigma_k)_{k=1}^{K}$ contains the GMM's parameters and $g(\mathbf{x}|\boldsymbol{\mu}, \Sigma)$ is a Gaussian with mean $\boldsymbol{\mu}$ and diagonal covariance matrix Σ. The parameters of the GMM are determined using expectation maximisation. Using the occurrence probabilities

$$\gamma_{kt} = \frac{\omega_k g(\mathbf{x}_t|\boldsymbol{\mu}_k, \Sigma_k)}{\sum_{j=1}^{K} \omega_j g(\mathbf{x}_t|\boldsymbol{\mu}_j, \Sigma_j)},$$

the $(2KD)$-dimensional descriptor (D is the dimension of the feature space) is built as $\mathbf{m} = \left(\mathbf{u}_1^\top, \ldots, \mathbf{u}_K^\top, \mathbf{v}_1^\top, \ldots, \mathbf{v}_K^\top\right)^\top$, where

$$\mathbf{u}_k = \frac{1}{N\sqrt{\omega_k}} \sum_{t=1}^{T} \gamma_{kt} \Sigma_k^{-\frac{1}{2}} (\mathbf{x}_t - \boldsymbol{\mu}_k), \text{and}$$

$$\mathbf{v}_k = \frac{1}{N\sqrt{2\omega_k}} \sum_{t=1}^{T} \gamma_{kt} \left[(\mathbf{x}_t - \boldsymbol{\mu}_k)^\top \Sigma_k^{-\frac{1}{2}} (\mathbf{x}_t - \boldsymbol{\mu}_k) - 1 \right].$$

2.1.3 Application in Visual Inspection

The fundamental requirements of automated visual inspection are quite different from other computer vision tasks such as image categorization. In some sense it is less difficult, since the environmental conditions – lighting, background, etc. – are tightly controlled. On the other hand, it is more difficult than other tasks: high throughput demands very short processing times. This prohibits usage of long processing pipelines and computation of complex feature descriptors such as SIFT. This suggests to divert from the usual path in two aspects: Dense sampling and usage of primitive feature descriptors.

In **dense sampling**, we consider every foreground-pixel (u, v) of an object as key-point where to extract the low level local feature descriptors. This has the benefit of skipping an interest point detection stage (thereby saving processing time), but is only feasible if the objects are relatively small and the descriptors themselves are inexpensive to compute. Hence, we use **primitive features** that require only very little processing time. In particular, the most basic descriptor is the color of a pixel, $\mathbf{x}_t = \mathcal{I}(u_t, v_t)$. Since K-means and GMM, like many other algorithms for cluster analysis, rely on measuring distances, the color space may have a significant impact on the discriminative ability of the object descriptor. To include other features, a D-channel local descriptor is constructed as $\mathbf{x}_t = (x_{1t}, \ldots, x_{Dt})^\top$, where each x_{dt} encodes a different feature-type. For example, x_{1t} to x_{3t} could correspond to the RGB values at the pixel (u_t, v_t). Texture is encoded e.g. using gradient magnitude, $x_{dt} = |\nabla\mathcal{I}(u_t, v_t)|$, rotation invariant uniform local binary patterns [OPM02] or center-symmetric local binary patterns [HPS06]. Finally, the shape of an object can be represented using the distance transform.

2.2 Local Descriptors

As BOV describes the object appearance as a whole, it does not provide information about the location of a defect. As a result, the method is unsuitable in situations where position is the major discriminative feature. In this section, we propose a novel method to learn descriptors that are able to describe such situations.

Similar to BOV, the descriptor is a collection of local features. However, instead of vectorial feature descriptors, we use very simple and *weak* binary features

$$f_n = \mathbf{1}\left[\phi_{n,1}(\mathbf{p}_{n,1}) - \phi_{n,2}(\mathbf{p}_{n,2}) < \tau_n\right], \tag{2.1}$$

where τ_n is a feature-specific threshold, $\phi(\mathbf{p})$ extracts some scalar features at the pixel at $\mathbf{p} = (u, v)$ and $\mathbf{1}[x]$ is the indicator function that is 1 if x is true and 0 otherwise. Note that neither necessarily $\mathbf{p}_{n,1} \neq \mathbf{p}_{n,2}$, nor $\phi_{n,1} = \phi_{n,2}$, which allows local features that evaluate the same pixel and features that compare different types of features.

The scalar features $\phi(\mathbf{p})$ are used to encode different aspects of the object and may be arbitrarily constructed. The only requirement is that the difference $(\phi(\mathbf{p}) - \phi(\mathbf{q}))$ is meaningful, that is ϕ should not extract some coding-scheme like LBP. However, as computation time is limited, simple extraction methods similar as the ones used in the BOV approach should be used. The hue or saturation at the location $\mathbf{p}$ can be used to represent the color of the object. Texture can be encoded using gray-value and gradient magnitude. Shape can again be encoded using the distance transform or the fraction of foreground-pixels in a region around $\mathbf{p}$. Similarly, the color and texture features can also be taken as the mean or other statistic in a region around $\mathbf{p}$. Finally, we suggest to normalize each feature to a value in $[0, 1]$. This ensures that the different channels are comparable.

To achieve invariance to rotation and scale, we index pixels relative to a local coordinate system (see Fig. 2.3): Given the center $\mathbf{c}$, major axis $\mathbf{b}_1$ and minor

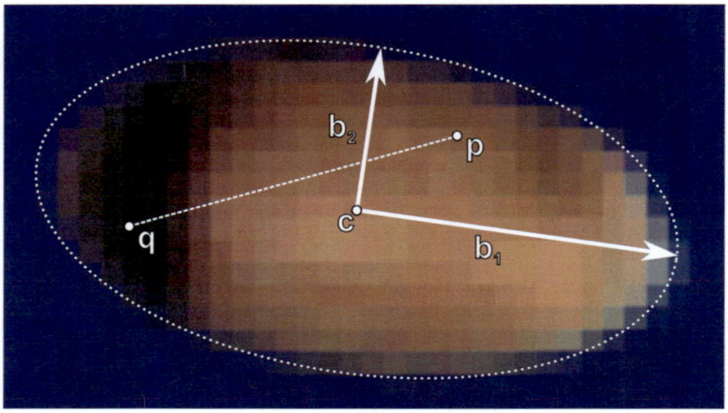

Figure 2.3: Local feature primitives comparing two locations in the image. Each feature is the difference of two descriptors extracted at two locations $\mathbf{p}$ and $\mathbf{q}$ in the object image. Invariance to rotation and scale is achieved by indexing relative to the object center $\mathbf{c}$ and the major and minor axes $\mathbf{b}_1$ and $\mathbf{b}_2$.

axis $\mathbf{b}_2$ of an object, the object indexed coordinates $\mathbf{x} = (\lambda, \mu)$ are transformed to global coordinates as $\mathbf{p} = \mathbf{c} + \lambda\mathbf{b}_1 + \mu\mathbf{b}_2$.

2.2.1 Feature Selection

The definition of these features leaves the question how to to learn discriminative descriptors. For this purpose, we adapt the random fern approach presented by Özuysal et al. [OCLF10]. A random fern F_m can be thought of as a collection of S binary features $f_i \in \{0, 1\}$, which divide the feature space into 2^S disjoint regions $\mathcal{R}_s$. Similar to decision and regression trees each $\mathcal{R}_s$ is associated with an output. In [OCLF10] the output of a single fern is a probability estimate $\hat{p}(c|\mathbf{f})$ that an object belongs to class c given the observations $\mathbf{f}$. The features in each fern are randomly selected. In this report, we propose to instead select the best from a pool of *feature candidates*.

Given a set of N training samples, we randomly sample K local coordinates $\mathbf{x} \in [-1, 1]^2$. Given L different feature extraction methods $\phi^{(l)}$, this produces a pool of $(LK)^2$ feature candidates. The best S features are selected in an iterative scheme, where in each round the feature combination that maximizes the correlation to an output value $\tilde{y}$ (see Algorithm 2.1),

$$\varrho(\phi_i - \phi_k, \tilde{y}) = \frac{\sum_{n=1}^{N}\left(\phi_i^{(n)} - \overline{\phi_i} - \phi_k^{(n)} + \overline{\phi_k}\right)\left(\tilde{y}^{(n)} - \overline{\tilde{y}}\right)}{\sqrt{\left(\sum_{n=1}^{N}\left(\phi_i^{(n)} - \overline{\phi_i} - \phi_k^{(n)} + \overline{\phi_k}\right)^2\right)\left(\sum_{n=1}^{N}\left(\tilde{y}^{(n)} - \overline{\tilde{y}}\right)^2\right)}}.$$

For the sake of brevity we abuse notation and write $\phi_i^{(n)}$ to denote the i-th combination of local coordinate and feature extraction method extracted from the n-th training sample, and $\overline{\phi_i}$ to denote the empirical mean over the samples (likewise for $\tilde{y}$). The threshold τ_n (see eq. (2.1)) is randomly selected in order to be more robust towards non-representative training sets. Finally, the binary feature $f_n = \mathbf{1}[\phi_i - \phi_k < \tau_n]$ is constructed and both ϕ_i and ϕ_k are removed from the pool of candidates. This process is continued until S features are selected.

The resulting random ferns are very fast to compute, but unable to reliably classify unknown objects. However, the combination of multiple ferns was proven to be a reliable classifier [OCLF10].

2.2.2 Fern Boosting

In the original paper, Özuysal et al. combined many random ferns in a semi-naive Bayesian method. However, since we are interested in a minimal number of ferns to keep the computational costs low, we propose to construct a cascade $F_M(\mathbf{x}) = \sum_{m=1}^{M} F_m(\mathbf{x})$ of random ferns using gradient boosting [Fri00]. Following Friedman, we adapt L_2_TreeBoost to employ random ferns instead of regression trees as weak classifiers. The modifications are straightforward, producing Algorithm 2.1.

Given the cascade $F_M(\mathbf{x})$, class membership probability estimates are derived as

$$\hat{p}(y = 1|\mathbf{x}) = \frac{1}{1 + \exp(-2F_M(\mathbf{x}))} \quad \text{and}$$
$$\hat{p}(y = -1|\mathbf{x}) = \frac{1}{1 + \exp(2F_M(\mathbf{x}))}.$$

Objects are classified according to

$$\hat{y}(\mathbf{x}) = 2 \cdot \mathbf{1}\big[c_- \, \hat{p}(y = 1|\mathbf{x}) > c_+ \, \hat{p}(y = -1|\mathbf{x})\big] - 1,$$

where c_- and c_+ are the costs of predicting $y = -1$ and $y = 1$ respectively when the true class is $y = 1$ resp. $y = -1$.

3 Conclusion

In this technical report, we proposed two methods of learning discriminative features for automated visual inspection from a sample of wanted and unwanted materials. The first method uses the bag of visual words framework to derive global

Algorithm 2.1 L_2_FernBost

Require: Number of iterations M, training set $\{\mathbf{x}^{(n)}, y^{(n)}\}_{n=1}^{N}$ with $y^{(n)} = \pm 1$

$$F_0(\mathbf{x}) = \frac{1}{2}\log\frac{1+\overline{y}}{1-\overline{y}}$$

for $m = 1, \ldots, M$ **do**

$$\tilde{y}^{(n)} = \frac{2y_i}{1+\exp\left(2y^{(n)}F_{m-1}(\mathbf{x}^{(n)})\right)} \quad \text{for} \quad n = 1, \ldots, N$$

$$\{\mathcal{R}_{ms}\}_1^{2^S} = \text{random-fern}(\{\mathbf{x}^{(n)}, \tilde{y}^{(n)}\}_{n=1}^{N}) \text{ with } S \text{ features}$$

$$\gamma_{ms} = \frac{\sum_{\mathbf{x}^{(n)}\in\mathcal{R}_{ms}} \tilde{y}^{(n)}}{\sum_{\mathbf{x}^{(n)}\in\mathcal{R}_{ms}} |\tilde{y}^{(n)}|(2-|\tilde{y}^{(n)}|)} \quad \text{for} \quad s = 1, \ldots, 2^S$$

$$F_m(\mathbf{x}) = F_{m-1}(\mathbf{x}) + \sum_{s=1}^{2^S} \gamma_{ms}\mathbf{1}[\mathbf{x}\in\mathcal{R}_{ms}]$$

end for

object descriptors that are invariant to both scale and rotation. The second method combines feature extraction and classification by learning a cascade of random ferns using gradient boosting. The features are sensitive to the defect's location and invariant to object scale and rotation due to the use of a local coordinate system.

Both methods allow to encode all major aspects of object appearance: color texture and shape. Both methods use very primitive underlying features such as the color of a pixel. Since they require only simple operations (sums, products and comparisons), both methods are very fast in operation. This comes at the cost of a lengthy (but automated) training phase.

In the future, we plan to evaluate both methods in different scenarios. The BOV approach is suited when the whole object appearance is of interest, e.g. in grading the ripeness of fruits. The cascade of random ferns will be evaluated on problems where the location of a defect is a major clue, for example in the detection of fungal infections in grains.

Bibliography

[BCGS+09] J. Blasco, S. Cubero, J. Gómez-Sanchís, P. Mira, and E. Moltó. Development of a machine for the automatic sorting of pomegranate (Punica granatum) arils based on computer vision. *Journal of Food Engineering*, 90(1):27–34, January 2009.

[BDLM00] L Bergasa, N Duffy, G Lacey, and M Mazo. Industrial inspection using Gaussian functions in a colour space. *Image and Vision Computing*, 18(12):951–957, September 2000.

[CDF+04] Gabriella Csurka, Christopher Dance, Lixin Fan, Jutta Willamowski, and Cédric Bray. Visual categorization with bags of keypoints. In *International Workshop on Statistical Learning in Computer Vision (ECCV)*, pages 1–22, 2004.

[DCL00] N. Duffy, J. Crowley, and G. Lacey. Object detection using colour. In *Proceedings 15th International Conference on Pattern Recognition. ICPR-2000*, volume 1, pages 700–703. IEEE Comput. Soc, 2000.

[DS06] Cheng-Jin Du and Da-Wen Sun. Learning techniques used in computer vision for food quality evaluation: a review. *Journal of Food Engineering*, 72(1):39–55, January 2006.

[Fri00] Jerome H Friedman. Greedy Function Approximation: A Gradient Boosting Machine. *Annals of Statistics*, 29:1189–1232, 2000.

[HPS06] Marko Heikkilä, Matti Pietikäinen, and Cordelia Schmid. Description of interest regions with center-symmetric local binary patterns. In *Computer Vision, Graphics and Image Processing*, pages 58–69. Springer, 2006.

[LCG09] Changyong Li, Qixin Cao, and Feng Guo. A method for color classification of fruits based on machine vision. *WSEAS TRANSACTIONS on SYSTEMS*, 8(2):312–321, February 2009.

[MPZ+03] Elias N Malamas, Euripides G.M Petrakis, Michalis Zervakis, Laurent Petit, and Jean-Didier Legat. A survey on industrial vision systems, applications and tools. *Image and Vision Computing*, 21(2):171–188, February 2003.

[OCLF10] Mustafa Özuysal, Michael Calonder, Vincent Lepetit, and Pascal Fua. Fast keypoint recognition using random ferns. *IEEE transactions on pattern analysis and machine intelligence*, 32(3):448–61, March 2010.

[OPM02] T. Ojala, M. Pietikainen, and T. Maenpaa. Multiresolution gray-scale and rotation invariant texture classification with local binary patterns. *IEEE Transactions on Pattern Analysis and Machine Intelligence*, 24(7):971–987, July 2002.

[PD07] Florent Perronnin and Christopher Dance. Fisher Kernels on Visual Vocabularies for Image Categorization. In *2007 IEEE Conference on Computer Vision and Pattern Recognition*, pages 1–8. IEEE, June 2007.

[RB14] Matthias Richter and Jürgen Beyerer. Parameter-learning for color sorting of bulk materials using genetic algorithms. In *Forum Bildverarbeitung 2014*, pages 107–118. KIT Scientific Publishing, 2014.

[ZLTL14] Dong Zhang, Dah-Jye Lee, Beau J. Tippetts, and Kirt D. Lillywhite. Date maturity and quality evaluation using color distribution analysis and back projection. *Journal of Food Engineering*, 131:161–169, June 2014.

Image Warping and Homogenization to Analyse the Frequency und Amplitude Modulation of Structural-Statistical Textures

Markus Vogelbacher

Vision and Fusion Laboratory
Institute for Anthropomatics
Karlsruhe Institute of Technology (KIT), Germany
markus.vogelbacher@kit.edu

Technical Report IES-2014-10

Abstract: Research is being conducted in the field of texture analysis for many years. In this process a wide variety of methods have been developed for analyzing and describing the various structural and statistical textures. For the complicated mixed case of structural-statistical textures only few methods exist which allow a general evaluation. One way to describe this texture type is to produce a deviation from a structural texture with the help of distortions and gray value differences. Inspired by the communication technology, this can be done with the help of frequency or amplitude modulations. In this report, an evaluation option for each type of modulation will be presented. Occurring geometric distortions can be described for example with the help of image warping algorithms. In this context, the retrieval of characteristic points of the texture primitive, i.e. recurrent points that are easy to detect, is an important and also challenging task. The detection of irregularities of the gray values over the entire texture can be achieved with the help of a image pre-processing method called homogenization. Thus, the combination of the two methods - image warping and homogenization - allows a complete description of the frequency and amplitude modulation of structural textures and provides a new way for the analysis of structural-statistical textures.

1 Introduction

Textures are all around us in everyday life. Whether it is the pattern of a carpet, the wood grain of a table or the nature of our clothing. Because almost each object has a texture it is beside the color and the shape one of the most important visual properties of an object. Thus, it is clear that the assessment of the texture represents also an important part of quality control, e.g. for industrial production. Although the term *texture* is commonly known, there is no generally accepted definition. Generally, textures can be described as two-dimensionl distinct structures with certain deterministic or statistical regularities. Depending on how much knowledge about the texture exists, basically three types of texture can be distinguished with no strict boundaries between the three types. Structural textures are characterized by a texture primitive that is repeated according to a fixed local arrangement scheme. In the area of structural-statistical textures the texture primitve and the arrangement scheme are both subject to stochastic fluctuations until finally in the area of statistical textures no more primitives can be identified.

Depending on which type of texture is present, there are different methods of analysis [HSD73, Har79, WH89, MJ92, RH99, GP03, Bey11]. These standard evaluation methods describe purely the structural or statistical properties of a texture. Only very few methods exist that attempt to describe the combined structural-statistical textures. In previous work [Hav96, Vog12, Vog13] these textures are described by amplitude or frequency modulation as known from the communication technology [Kam11]. A variation of the gray value corresponds to an amplitude modulation (AM) and the changes in the shape of the primitive or the arrangement scheme corresponds to a frequency modulation (FM). The determination of the appropriate modulation is achieved by consideration of the frequency spectrum [Hav96] or by a phase locked loop [Vog12, Vog13]. In this report, alternative ways to establish the parameters of the amplitude and the frequency modulation are presented. These enable the demodulation with homogenization (Section 2) and image warping (Section 3) and allow a complete analysis of structural-statistical textures.

2 Description of the Amplitude Modulation with Homogenization

The variation of the gray value and thus the AM can be obtained with the help of methods from image enhancement. A method exactly for this application is called *homogenization*, which is used to compensate illumination inhomogeneities in images.

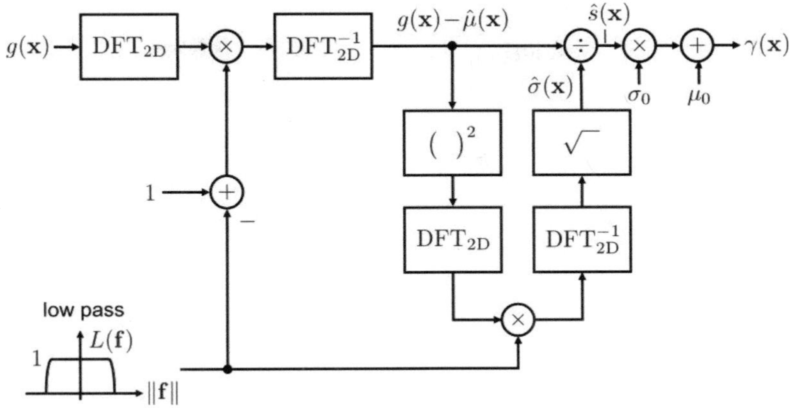

Figure 2.1: AM Demodulation with homogenization of the 2nd degree [Bey11]. $g(\mathbf{x})$: gray value at position $\mathbf{x}$, $\widehat{\sigma}(\mathbf{x})$, $\widehat{\mu}(\mathbf{x})$: estimated local contrast and mean, $\widehat{s}(\mathbf{x})$: adjusted texture (with mean value zero), DFT: discrete Fourier transform, $\gamma(\mathbf{x})$: adjusted texture containing the constants σ_0 and μ_0 for the conversion into a displayable grayscale image.

2.1 Homogenization for Image Pre-Processing

For the homogenization basically two models can be distinguished, depending on the degree of detail:

1. Degree: $g(\mathbf{x}) = t(\mathbf{x}) + b(\mathbf{x})$
2. Degree: $g(\mathbf{x}) = \sigma(\mathbf{x}) \cdot t(\mathbf{x}) + \mu(\mathbf{x})$

Thereby $\mathbf{x} = (x_1, x_2)$ describes a point in the two-dimensional space. Both models include a locally fast variable part, the desired texture $t(\mathbf{x})$, and a locally slowly variable part of inhomogeneities containing the desired AM $b(\mathbf{x})$. Below the 2nd degree model is used to describe the AM. Thus, the locally slowly variable AM is split into a local contrast $\sigma(\mathbf{x})$ and a local mean $\mu(\mathbf{x})$. Compared to the 1st degree model, where a simple low pass filtering is sufficient for demodulation, the demodulation of the 2nd degree model is much more complex. In Fig. 2.1 the procedure for estimating the parameters is explained in a diagram. Using high and low pass filtering, the local contrast and the local mean of the AM can be determined and thus the adjusted texture $\widehat{s}(\mathbf{x})$ obtained [Bey11].

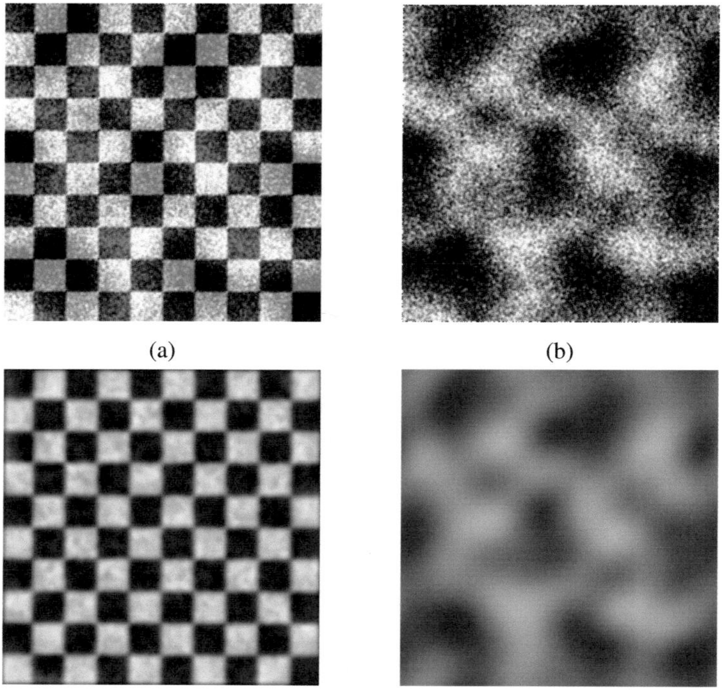

(a) (b) (c) (d)

Figure 2.2: Example for the demodulation of an amplitude modulated texture by homogenization. (a) modulated chess board pattern, (b) real artificial AM, (c) adjusted texture and (d) AM determined from $\widehat{\sigma}(\mathbf{x})$ of the homogenization.

2.2 Results

Fig. 2.2 shows an example of demodulating an amplitude modulated texture, in this case a chess board pattern (Fig. 2.2(a)). The artificially applied AM (Fig. 2.2(b)) can be obtained with the help of the $\widehat{\sigma}(\mathbf{x})$ and $\widehat{\mu}(\mathbf{x})$ parameters of the homogenization from the modulated texture (Fig. 2.2(d)). In the resulting adjusted texture (Fig. 2.2(c)) only possible frequency modulations remain, which are discussed in the following Section 3. In most instances the information about the real AM of a modulated texture doesn't exist. For this reason the assessment of the quality of the estimation of the AM is limited to a visual comparison, as shown in Fig. 2.2.

3 Description of the Frequency Modulation with Image Warping

As described in the introduction, the FM of textures can be described as changes in the shape of the primitive or the arrangement scheme. One method that allows a description of the changes from a structural texture to a frequency modulated texture and thus an assessment of the changes in the structural arrangement scheme is *image warping*, which is commonly used in image editing.

3.1 Image Warping Basics

Image warping is a transformation that influences the geometrical characteristics of an image. Ideally, the intensity of the warped image I' at the position $\mathbf{q} = (x, y)$ corresponds to the intensity of the original image I at the corresponding position $\mathbf{p} = (u, v)$, so that $\mathbf{q} = f(\mathbf{p})$. It means that $I'(\mathbf{q}) = I(\mathbf{p})$ or $I'(f(\mathbf{p})) = I(\mathbf{p})$. For the consideration of the FM, the frequency modulated or distorted texture is assumed as the warped image I', which is the original image I arisen by a displacement field $f(\cdot)$ from the structural texture. In the application of image warping, global (affine, perspective, bilinear, polynomial, ...) and local transformation, e.g. piecewise affine transformations, can be distinguished [GM98]. Local transforms are especially interesting for the application FM, because local changes should be considered. For this purpose the image is divided into several smaller sub-images and subsequently transformed separately affine. There are different methods to ensure this division into sub-images. For example by defining point sets followed by a connection to a network, which is called *mesh warping* or by defining lines that affect a particular image region at the transformation, which is called *field morphing* or *featured based warping* [Wol98].

3.2 Image Warping Algorithm for Frequency Modulation

For the assessment of the frequency modulation, the mesh warping principle is used, because it allows an easy describtion of local changes. For this, it is necessary to detect distinctive points of the basic primitive at first. In the next step, the corresponding points between the ideal structural and the distorted texture must be detected over the entire texture to subsequently generate from this set of points a grid and to specify the piecewise affine transformations. The principle of assignment of corresponding points is illustrated in Fig. 3.1 on the distortion of a chess board pattern. The detection of feature points can be done by known methods such

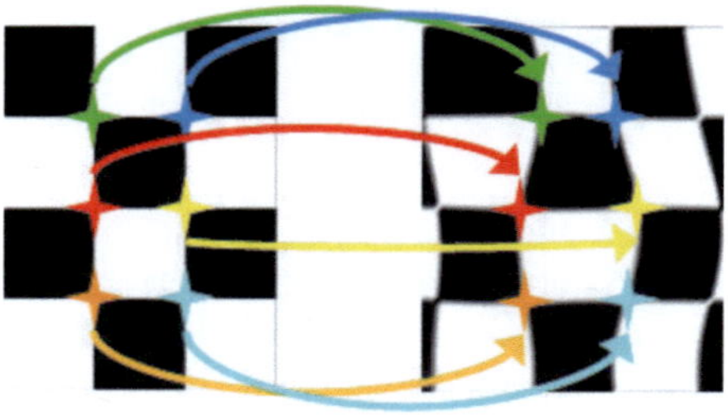

Figure 3.1: Example for the allocation of corresponding points between the ideal structural (I, left) and distorted (I', right) texture.

as Harris/Shi-Tomasi corner detector, SIFT, SURF, FAST, BRIEF or ORB [ML12]. The network, which should be obtained from the feature points can be created with triangles for example using the Delaunay triangulation [LS80]. The summary of each piecewise affine transformations ultimately leads to the displacement field for the description of the FM.

3.3 Upcoming Problems Using Image Warping Algorithm

Several problems may occur in the procedure desribed in Section 3.2. On the one hand, in the search for feature points, points may be lost or new points appear due to the distortions occuring in the modulated texture. This leads to a loss of corresponding points, thus to incorrect assignments and to an erroneous displacement field. Also in the net mesh generation using the *Delaunay* triangulation, different formations of the net meshes can occur because of the changing distances between the feature points due to the distortions. This leads to different net meshes when comparing the ideal structural and the distorted texture, thus again to incorrect assignments and an erroneous displacement field. These problems could be solved for example with more robust methods, which exploit neighborhood relations. Therefore, in the basic texture primitve certain points should be retrieved, which have a fixed geometric relationship to each other. This would also create a unique mesh generation. Distortions leading to disappearing feature points or completely unrecognizable primitves, can not be covered by any improvement of the process.

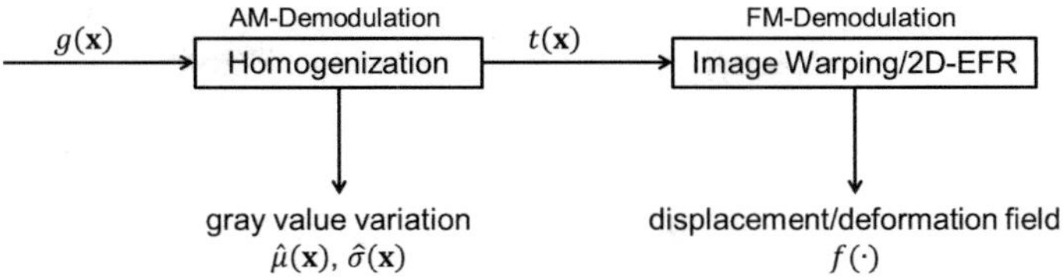

Figure 4.1: Complete system for AM-FM demodulation of structural-statistical textures. $g(\mathbf{x})$: amplitude and frequency modulated texture, $\widehat{\sigma}(\mathbf{x})$, $\widehat{\mu}(\mathbf{x})$: parameters of the AM, $t(\mathbf{x})$: purely frequency modulated texture, $f(\cdot)$: displacement/deformation field.

4 Conclusion

This report deals with the description of structural-statistical textures using the modulation approach of communications technology. Therefore, the variation of the gray value or the variation of the basic primitive or the arrangement scheme can be considered as amplitude or frequency modulation.

For the two types of modulation, respectively, two methods for demodulation were presented. Parameters for amplitude modulation could be exported out of the homogenization of the modulated texture. The frequency modulation can be described using the image warping approach. However, it has been postulated that some problems hamper the accurate determination of the displacement field. These known problems must be brought under control in future work. The determination of the frequnecy modulation may alternatively be achieved with the help of a two-dimensional expanded Fourier series (2D-EFR), as described in [Vog13].

Overall, this can be seen as an approach to allow a complete analysis of structural-statistical texture (Fig. 4.1) in further work.

Bibliography

[Bey11] J. Beyerer. Lecture: Automatische Sichtprüfung und Bildverarbeitung. *Karlsruher Institut für Technologie, Lehrstuhl für Interaktive Echtzeitsysteme*, 2011.

[GM98] C.A. Glasbey and K.V. Mardia. A review of image warping methods. *Journal of Applied Statistics*, 25:155–171, 1998.

[GP03] S.E. Grigorescu and N. Petkov. Texture analysis using Renyi's generalized entropies. *International Conference on Image Processing*, 2003.

[Har79] R.M. Haralick. Statistical and structural approaches to texture. *Proceedings of the IEEE*, 67(5):786 – 804, 1979.

[Hav96] J.P. Havlicek. *AM-FM Image Models*. PhD thesis, The University of Texas at Austin, 1996.

[HSD73] R.M. Haralick, K. Shanmugam, and I. Dinstein. Textural features for image classification. *IEEE Transactions on Systems, Man and Cybernetics*, SMC-3(6):610–621, 1973.

[Kam11] K.D. Kammeyer. *Nachrichtenübertragung*. Vieweg+Teubner Verlag, 2011.

[LS80] D.T. Lee and B.J. Schachter. Two algorithms for constructing a Delauny triangulation. *International Journal of Computer and Information Sciences*, 9:219–242, 1980.

[MJ92] J. Mao and A.K. Jain. Texture classification and segmentation using multiresolution simultaneous autoregressive models. *Pattern Recognition*, 25(2):173–188, 1992.

[ML12] M. Muja and D.G. Lowe. Fast matching of binary features. *Ninth Conference on Computer and Robot Vision*, pages 404–410, 2012.

[RH99] T. Randen and J.H. Husoy. Filtering for texture classification: A comparative study. *IEEE Transactions on Pattern Analysis and Machine Intelligence*, 21(4):291–310, 1999.

[Vog12] M. Vogelbacher. Review and outlook for texture analysis methods. Technical report, Vision and Fusion Laboratory, Institute for Anthropomatics, Karlsruhe Institute of Technology (KIT), 2012.

[Vog13] M. Vogelbacher. Review and outlook for texture analysis methods a texture modulation model to describe structural-statistical textures. Technical report, Vision and Fusion Laboratory, Institute for Anthropomatics, Karlsruhe Institute of Technology (KIT), 2013.

[WH89] L. Wang and D.C. He. Texture classification using texture spectrum. *Pattern Recognition*, 23(8):905–910, 1989.

[Wol98] G. Wolberg. Image morphing: a survey. *The Visual Computer*, 14:360–372, 1998.

Defect perception thresholds on specular surfaces

Mathias Ziebarth

Vision and Fusion Laboratory
Institute for Anthropomatics and Robotics
Karlsruhe Institute of Technology, Germany
mathias.ziebarth@kit.edu

Technical Report IES-2014-11

Abstract: Today, measurement methods like deflectometry allow accurate measurements of specular surfaces. The measurement methods are often more precise than human vision. If the aim is to inspect surfaces for defects that would disturb humans, so called aesthetic defects, it is important to understand the connection between the measurement method and human vision. This problem is addressed in this report. In contrast to matte surfaces, there are different influencing factors for the perception of specular surfaces. We are proposing a model which introduces a lower bound for the visibility of defects on specular surfaces. This means that defects smaller than this bound cannot be identified by an average human observer.

1 Introduction

The automated visual inspection of specular surfaces is a practical problem with many applications. Today, there are methods known to get precise measurements of specular surfaces, ranging from small glossy mobile devices up to large lacquered automobile bodies. One way to acquire the surface shape is a measurement method called deflectometry, which can be used for specular to partially specular surfaces. It has the advantage of being especially sensitive to changes in the surface gradient. This corresponds to the human perception of specular surfaces. When surfaces which have to "look good" are inspected, all defects visible to a human under defined conditions should be detected. Therefore the defects are defined by some aesthetical measure, which depends on the human visual system, surface properties and a typical environment. In this paper we propose such an approach to quantify the visibility of aesthetic defects. For this purpose we define thresholds for the visibility of defects on specular surfaces. Defects smaller than these quantifications are invisible for an average human observer.

2 Related Work

Some work was done to automatically assess specular surfaces as humans would do. First of all, Hsakou [Hsa06] uses deflectometry and makes use of the surface curvature for assessment, as it correlates to human visual inspection. Additional decision criteria like location, area, amplitude and density are identified by comparing automated with manual inspections. Finally, tolerance thresholds for combinations of the identified criteria are chosen assisted by an inspector.

The detection, classification and evaluation of surface defects is a rather general task with many applications and accordingly a lot of studies exist in this field. The studied applications range from the evaluation of auto-body panels [And09, Fer13], assessing scratch damages in bulk materials and coatings [HWP03], scratch visibility on polymers [RSW$^+$03, JBH$^+$10, LBS$^+$11] and defects on machined and painted surfaces [PK06].

3 Derivation of the model

In this section we derive the model which connects the influencing factors with the minimum defect sizes visible for a human observer.

3.1 Resolution on the surface

Given the variables angular resolution θ, incident angle on the surface α and the viewing distance to the surface d we want to determine the resolution on the surface a as shown in Fig. 3.1:

$$\frac{a}{\sin(\theta)} = \frac{d'}{\sin(\alpha')}, \tag{3.1}$$

$$\alpha' = \alpha - \frac{\theta}{2}, \tag{3.2}$$

$$\frac{d'}{\sin(\alpha)} = \frac{d}{\sin(180 - \alpha - \frac{\theta}{2})}.$$

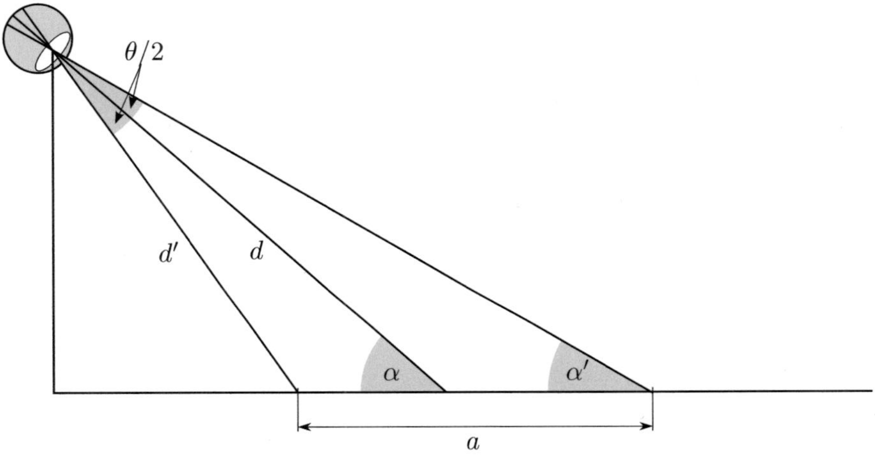

Figure 3.1: Lateral resolution on the surface.

Using the symmetry of the sine function $\sin(180 - x) = \sin(x)$ we get

$$d' = \frac{d\sin(\alpha)}{\sin(\alpha + \frac{\theta}{2})}. \tag{3.3}$$

Inserting (3.2) and (3.3) in (3.1) we obtain

$$a = \frac{d\sin(\theta)\sin(\alpha)}{\sin(\alpha - \frac{\theta}{2})\sin(\alpha + \frac{\theta}{2})}. \tag{3.4}$$

Using the sinus law $\sin(x)\sin(y) = \frac{1}{2}(\cos(x-y) - \cos(x+y))$ and the asymmetry of the cosine function $\cos(x) = \cos(-x)$ (3.4) can be simplified to

$$a = 2d\frac{\sin(\theta)\sin(\alpha)}{\cos(\theta) - \cos(2\alpha)}. \tag{3.5}$$

In the special case of $\alpha = 90$ (3.5) simplifies to

$$\begin{aligned} a &= 2d\frac{\sin(\theta)}{\cos(\theta) + 1} \\ &= 2d\tan(\frac{\theta}{2}). \end{aligned}$$

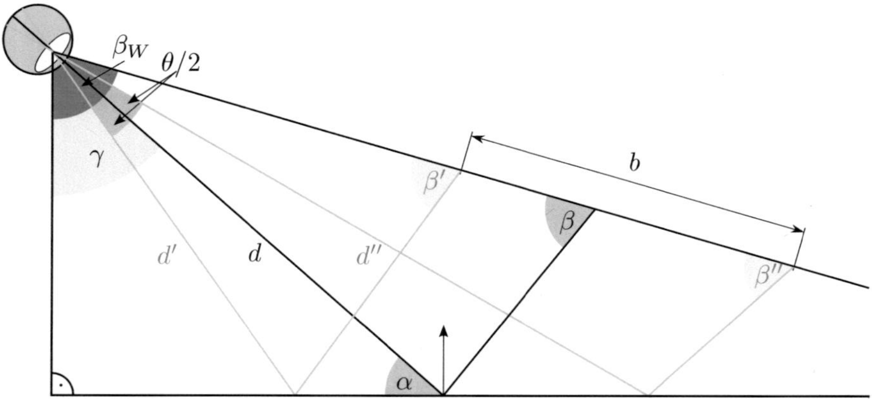

Figure 3.2: Angular resolution caused by resolution on the screen.

3.2 Resolution on the screen

Similar to section 3.1 in (3.5) and using the variables angular resolution θ, incident angle on the screen β and the viewing distance from the observer over the surface to the screen $d + h$ we determine the resolution on the screen b as in Fig. 3.2:

$$b = 2(d+h)\frac{\sin(\theta)\sin(\beta)}{\cos(\theta) - \cos(2\beta)}. \tag{3.6}$$

In the special case of $\beta = 90$ (3.6) simplifies to

$$b = 2(d+h)\tan(\frac{\theta}{2}).$$

3.3 Deflection on the screen

Similar to the previous sections 3.1 and 3.2 as in (3.5) and (3.6) and using the variables surface normal change $\Delta\phi$, incident angle on the screen β and the distance from the surface to the screen h we determine the deflection of the viewing rays on the screen c as in Fig. 3.3:

$$c = 2h\frac{\sin(\Delta\phi)\sin(\beta)}{\cos(\Delta\phi) - \cos(2\beta)}. \tag{3.7}$$

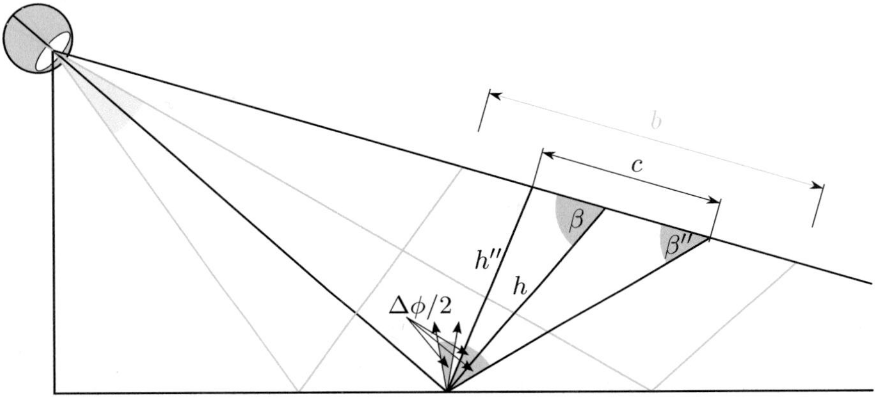

Figure 3.3: Deflection on the screen caused by change of the surface normal.

In the special case of $\beta = 90$ (3.7) simplifies to

$$c = 2h\tan(\Delta\phi).$$

3.4 Defect model triangle

Assuming a triangular shaped defect as in Fig. 3.4, we need the variable $\Delta\phi$ for the triangle gradient and a_t for the lateral extend of the defect to obtain the defect depth t

$$a_t = \frac{t}{\tan(\frac{\Delta\phi}{2})}. \tag{3.8}$$

3.5 Deviation

A defect on the surface is visible if two conditions are met. At first the observer has to be able to resolve the defect on the surface $a = a_t$ using (3.5) and (3.8), which leads to

$$2d\frac{\sin(\theta)\sin(\alpha)}{\cos(\theta) - \cos(2\alpha)} = \frac{t}{\tan(\frac{\Delta\phi}{2})}. \tag{3.9}$$

In the special case of $\alpha = \beta = 90$ (3.9) simplifies to

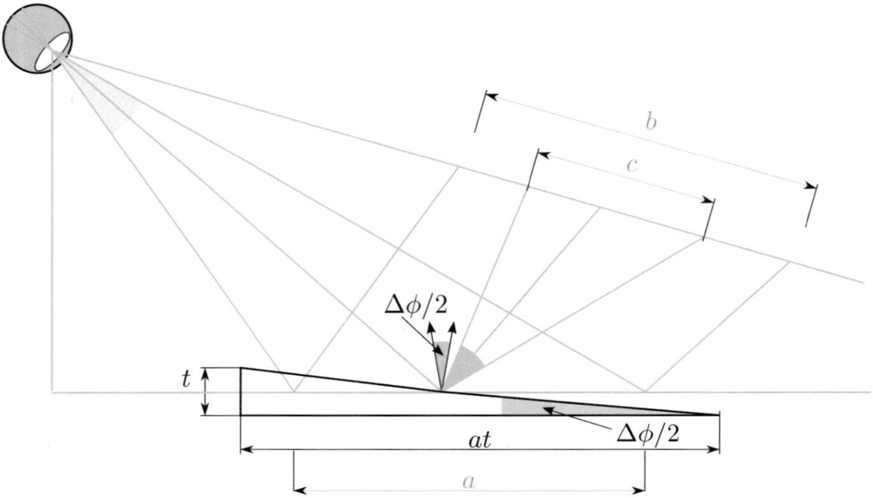

Figure 3.4: Triangular defect model causes deflection of viewing rays.

$$2d\tan(\frac{\theta}{2}) = 2h\tan(\Delta\phi). \quad (3.10)$$

The second condition is that the deflection has to be resolved on the screen $b = c$ using (3.6) and (3.7)

$$2(d+h)\frac{\sin(\theta)\sin(\beta)}{\cos(\theta)-\cos(2\beta)} = 2h\frac{\sin(\Delta\phi)\sin(\beta)}{\cos(\Delta\phi)-\cos(2\beta)}. \quad (3.11)$$

In the special case of $\alpha = \beta = 90$ (3.11) simplifies to

$$2(d+h)\tan(\frac{\theta}{2}) = 2h\tan(\Delta\phi),$$

which leads to

$$\Delta\phi = \arctan(\frac{d+h}{h}\tan(\frac{\theta}{2})). \quad (3.12)$$

Inserting (3.12) into (3.10) we get

$$2(d+h)\tan(\frac{\theta}{2}) = \frac{t}{\frac{d+h}{h}\tan(\frac{\theta}{2})}$$

and hence

$$t = 2(d+h)\frac{d}{h}\tan^2(\frac{\theta}{2}).$$

As it can be observed that the angle $\Delta\phi$ is nearly 0, we can approximate $\tan(\Delta\phi) \approx \Delta\phi$, so analogue to (3.12) we can write $\Delta\phi$ without assuming $\alpha = \beta = 90$ as

$$\Delta\phi = \frac{2\sin^2(\beta)(d+h)\sin(\theta)}{(d+h)\sin(\theta) - h\cos(2\beta) + h\cos(\theta)}. \tag{3.13}$$

Inserting (3.13) into (3.5) and using the triangle defect model from (3.8) we get

$$t = -\frac{2d\sin(\alpha)\sin(\theta)\tan\left(\frac{\sin^2(\beta)(d+h)\sin(\theta)}{(d+h)\sin(\theta)-h\cos(2\beta)+h\cos(\theta)}\right)}{\cos(2\alpha) - \cos(\theta)}. \tag{3.14}$$

The proposed model (3.14) gives the lower bound for the visibility of a defect on a specular surface. For the defect we assume a triangular shape (3.8) that deflects one viewing ray on a screen. With an appropriate pattern this deflection can be resolved. Furthermore the defect itself has to be large enough to be resolved on the surface, as given in (3.5).

4 Results & Discussion

Before evaluating the model derived above, it is necessary to define the viewing capabilities of an average human observer and a typical surrounding. We describe the viewing capability with the angular resolution of the human eye and assume an observer with the average visual acuity of $\theta = \frac{1}{60}^\circ$ [PPBS08]. The visual acuity describes the spatial resolution of the human eye, especially the ability to discriminate between two separate points. Furthermore as typical environment for the observation we have chosen a car dealership with viewing distances ranging from $d_{\text{min}} = \frac{30}{100}m$ to $d_{\text{max}} = 2m$ and screen distances ranging from $h_{\text{min}} = 1m$ to $d_{\text{max}} = 10m$. The screen has to show patterns that allow the detection of very small deflections of viewing rays.

As a first result, Figure 4.1 shows the minimal visible width by evaluating (3.5) with $\alpha = 90$. Figure 4.2 shows the minimal visible height by evaluating (3.14) with $\alpha = \beta = 90$ and Figure 4.3 shows the minimal visible height by evaluating (3.14) with minimal viewing distance d_{min} and maximal screen distance h_{max}.

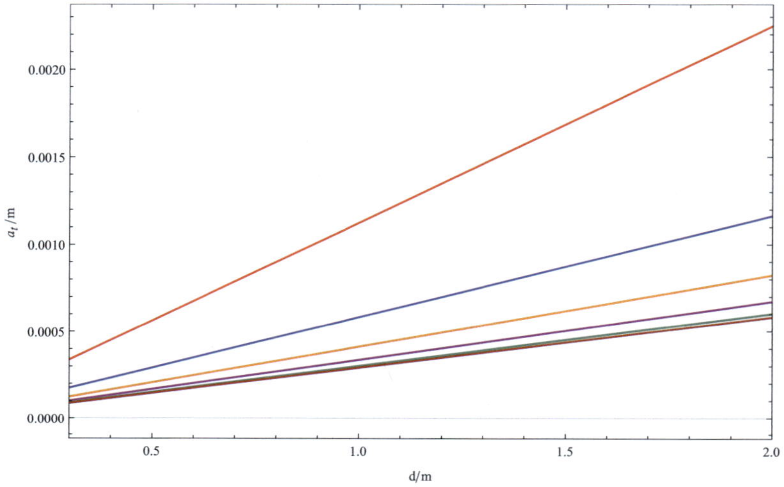

Figure 4.1: Minimal visible defect width a_t with respect to viewing distance d for several incident angles on the surface α.

Looking at (3.14) it can be seen that for minimal viewing distance d_{min} and maximal screen distance h_{max} the smallest defects are visible. Under these optimal viewing conditions, a defect may be as small as $87\mu m$ in lateral extend, 0.01 steepness and $32nm$ in height. One drawback of the model is that the lateral extend and steepness of the defect are linked. Thus defects with the same height have a larger gradient when their lateral extend is smaller, which does not correspond to the intuition that small changes in height are better visible when the defect has a large extend. Another drawback is that we only look at the first derivative of the surface, which is responsible for the deviation of single viewing rays. Usually humans are used to observe distortions of known patterns, which corresponds to the second derivative of the surface. Also it results in reducing the capabilities of the human eye to just one value, the visual acuity. Areal pattern resolution capabilties are ignored.

5 Conclusion

We proposed a model to estimate lower bounds for the visibility of defects on specular surfaces. Therefore a perfect specularity, a triangle shaped defect and an optimal pattern on the screen were assumed. The benefit of the model is that the visibility is attributed to known quantities such as the visual acuity of the human

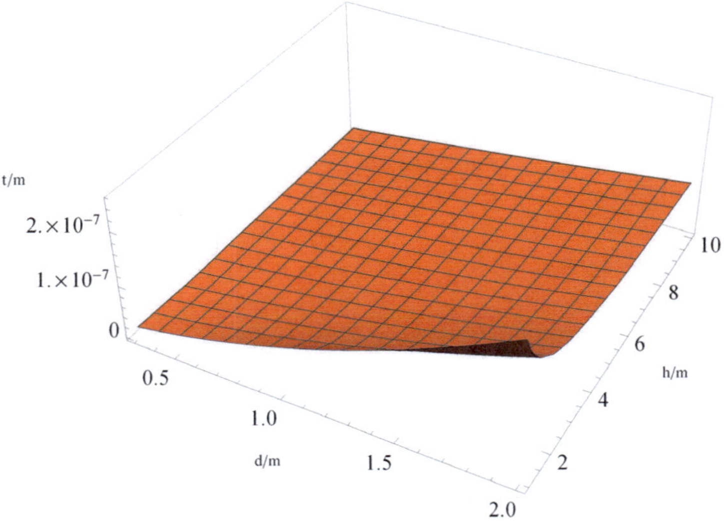

Figure 4.2: Minimal visible defect height with respect to viewing distance d and screen distance h and incident angles on the surface and the screen of $\alpha = \beta = 90$.

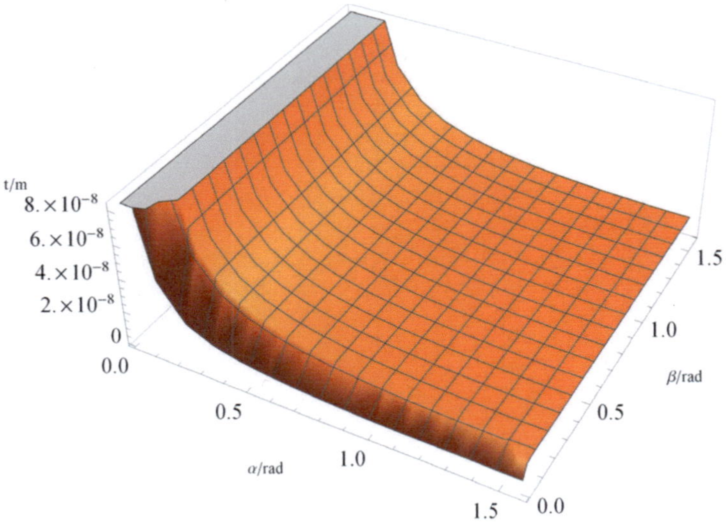

Figure 4.3: Minimal visible defect height with respect to incident viewing angle α and screen angle β and for minimal viewing distance d and maximal screen distance h.

eye, observation angles and distances. Assuming an average acuity under optimal viewing conditions the model gives very small lower boundaries for the visibility of defects. The lower bounds obtained with this model are very small, but as the model makes some artificial worst case assumptions such as a perfect specular surface and a perfect pattern, the results should get more practical as more realistic assumptions are included in the model.

Bibliography

[And09] A. Andersson. Evaluation and visualisation of surface defects on auto-body panels . *Journal of Materials Processing Technology*, 209(2):821–837, 2009.

[Fer13] K. Fernholz. Quantifying the Visibility of Surface Distortions in Class "A" Automotive Exterior Body Panels. *Journal of Manufacturing Science and Engineering*, 135:011001–1, 2013.

[Hsa06] Réda Hsakou. Curvature: the relevant criterion for class-a surface quality. *JEC Composites Magazine*, pages 105–108, March 2006.

[HWP03] I. Hutchings, P. Wang, and G. Parry. An optical method for assessing scratch damage in bulk materials and coatings. *Surface and Coatings Technology*, 165(2):186–193, 2003.

[JBH+10] H. Jiang, R. Browning, M. Hossain, H-J. Sue, and M. Fujiwara. Quantitative evaluation of scratch visibility resistance of polymers. *Applied Surface Science*, 256(21):6324–6329, 2010.

[LBS+11] P. Liu, R. Browning, H-J. Sue, J. Li, and S. Jones. Quantitative scratch visibility assessment of polymers based on Erichsen and ASTM/ISO scratch testing methodologies. *Polymer Testing*, 30(6):633–640, 2011.

[PK06] F. Puente León and S. Kammel. Inspection of specular and painted surfaces with centralized fusion techniques. *Measurement*, 39(6):536–546, 2006.

[PPBS08] F. Pedrotti, L. Pedrotti, W. Bausch, and H. Schmidt. *Optik für Ingenieure*. Springer Berlin Heidelberg, 2008.

[RSW+03] P. Rangarajan, M. Sinha, V. Watkins, K. Harding, and J. Sparks. Scratch visibility of polymers measured using optical imaging. *Polymer Engineering & Science*, 43(3):749–758, 2003.

Karlsruher Schriftenreihe zur Anthropomatik (ISSN 1863-6489)

Herausgeber: Prof. Dr.-Ing. Jürgen Beyerer

Die Bände sind unter www.ksp.kit.edu als PDF frei verfügbar oder als Druckausgabe bestellbar.

Band 1 Jürgen Geisler
Leistung des Menschen am Bildschirmarbeitsplatz. 2006
ISBN 3-86644-070-7

Band 2 Elisabeth Peinsipp-Byma
Leistungserhöhung durch Assistenz in interaktiven Systemen zur Szenenanalyse. 2007
ISBN 978-3-86644-149-1

Band 3 Jürgen Geisler, Jürgen Beyerer (Hrsg.)
Mensch-Maschine-Systeme. 2010
ISBN 978-3-86644-457-7

Band 4 Jürgen Beyerer, Marco Huber (Hrsg.)
Proceedings of the 2009 Joint Workshop of Fraunhofer IOSB and Institute for Anthropomatics, Vision and Fusion Laboratory. 2010
ISBN 978-3-86644-469-0

Band 5 Thomas Usländer
Service-oriented design of environmental information systems. 2010
ISBN 978-3-86644-499-7

Band 6 Giulio Milighetti
Multisensorielle diskret-kontinuierliche Überwachung und Regelung humanoider Roboter. 2010
ISBN 978-3-86644-568-0

Band 7 Jürgen Beyerer, Marco Huber (Hrsg.)
Proceedings of the 2010 Joint Workshop of Fraunhofer IOSB and Institute for Anthropomatics, Vision and Fusion Laboratory. 2011
ISBN 978-3-86644-609-0

Band 8 Eduardo Monari
Dynamische Sensorselektion zur auftragsorientierten Objektverfolgung in Kameranetzwerken. 2011
ISBN 978-3-86644-729-5

Band 9	Thomas Bader **Multimodale Interaktion in Multi-Display-Umgebungen.** 2011 ISBN 3-86644-760-8
Band 10	Christian Frese **Planung kooperativer Fahrmanöver für kognitive Automobile.** 2012 ISBN 978-3-86644-798-1
Band 11	Jürgen Beyerer, Alexey Pak (Hrsg.) **Proceedings of the 2011 Joint Workshop of Fraunhofer IOSB and Institute for Anthropomatics, Vision and Fusion Laboratory.** 2012 ISBN 978-3-86644-855-1
Band 12	Miriam Schleipen **Adaptivität und Interoperabilität von Manufacturing Execution Systemen (MES).** 2013 ISBN 978-3-86644-955-8
Band 13	Jürgen Beyerer, Alexey Pak (Hrsg.) **Proceedings of the 2012 Joint Workshop of Fraunhofer IOSB and Institute for Anthropomatics, Vision and Fusion Laboratory.** 2013 ISBN 978-3-86644-988-6
Band 14	Hauke-Hendrik Vagts **Privatheit und Datenschutz in der intelligenten Überwachung: Ein datenschutzgewährendes System, entworfen nach dem „Privacy by Design" Prinzip.** 2013 ISBN 978-3-7315-0041-4
Band 15	Christian Kühnert **Data-driven Methods for Fault Localization in Process Technology.** 2013 ISBN 978-3-7315-0098-8
Band 16	Alexander Bauer **Probabilistische Szenenmodelle für die Luftbildauswertung.** 2014 ISBN 978-3-7315-0167-1
Band 17	Jürgen Beyerer, Alexey Pak (Hrsg.) **Proceedings of the 2013 Joint Workshop of Fraunhofer IOSB and Institute for Anthropomatics, Vision and Fusion Laboratory.** 2014 ISBN 978-3-7315-0212-8
Band 18	Michael Teutsch **Moving Object Detection and Segmentation for Remote Aerial Video Surveillance.** 2015 ISBN 978-3-7315-0320-0

Band 19 Marco Huber
Nonlinear Gaussian Filtering:
Theory, Algorithms, and Applications. 2015
ISBN 978-3-7315-0338-5

Band 20 Jürgen Beyerer, Alexey Pak (Hrsg.)
Proceedings of the 2014 Joint Workshop of Fraunhofer IOSB and Institute for Anthropomatics, Vision and Fusion Laboratory. 2014
ISBN 978-3-7315-0401-6